JONATHAN BARDON was born
the High School Dublin, at 1
University Belfast. He has livec
at the Belfast Institute of Furth
Faculty Adviser. He has scripte
chairman of the Community Relations Council.

His publications include: *The Struggle for Ireland: 400–1450 AD* (1970); *Belfast: An Illustrated History* (1982); *Dublin: One Thousand Years of Wood Quay* (1984); *Belfast: 1000 Years* (1985); *If Ever You Go To Dublin Town: A Historic Guide to the City's Street Names* (with Carol Bardon) (1988); *Investigating Place Names in Ulster: A Teacher's Guide* (1991): *A History of Ulster* (1992); and *A Shorter Illustrated History of Ulster* (1996).

DAVID BURNETT was born in Lurgan, County Armagh, in 1971 and was educated at Lurgan College and at Queen's University Belfast where he gained a Ph.D. in Modern History. He now lives in Chelmsford, Essex, where he works as a teacher.

JONATHAN BARDON

DAVID BURNETT

•

BELFAST

A Pocket History

THE
BLACKSTAFF
PRESS

BELFAST

ACKNOWLEDGEMENTS

Grateful acknowledgement is made to the Belfast Central
Library, the Belfast Harbour Commissioners, the *Belfast
Telegraph*, Brian Hughes, the Linen Hall Library, the
Northern Ireland Housing Executive, Pacemaker Press
International, the Deputy Keeper of the Public Record
Office of Northern Ireland, Shorts plc, the Ulster Folk and
Transport Museum, the Ulster Museum, the Ulster Society,
and Brian Walker.

First published in 1996 by
The Blackstaff Press Limited
3 Galway Park, Dundonald, Belfast BT16 0AN, Northern Ireland

© Jonathan Bardon and David Burnett, 1996
All rights reserved

Typeset by Techniset Typesetters, Newton-le-Willows, Merseyside

Printed in Ireland by ColourBooks Limited

A CIP catalogue record for this book
is available from the British Library

ISBN 0-85640-588-4

CONTENTS

for Nicola,
Emily, Jimmy and Steven
DB

1
EARLY TIMES

Geography and natural resources do not account for the growth of Belfast. Much of the land is low-lying, prone to flooding, and composed of muddy shingle, clay and sand, providing an uncertain base for buildings, as the leaning Albert Clock indicates. And though local clay made the bricks used to construct nearly all the city's dwellings, those bricks had to be fired with imported British coal. On a still day, smoke and fumes from houses and industry hang captured by the semicircle of hills that surround the city. Indeed, the site was so unattractive that the development of a town at the mouth of the River Lagan was not begun until the seventeenth century. The settlement of Belfast, like its development, is primarily a story of people rather than place.

The Celtic-speaking Irish or Erinn, who dominated early Christian Ireland, used this area as a ford and named it Béal Feirsde: literally, the mouth of, or approach to, the sandbank or crossing. According to the Annals of Tighernach, the local Irish warrior clan, the Ulaid, fought the Cruithin, a people closely linked to the Picts of northern Britain, at a place it called the 'Fearsat' in AD 666. As the Annals of Ulster explained later, in the fifteenth century, 'the Fearsat here alluded to was evidently at Belfast on the river Lagan'. Belfast had its first mention in history. Viking raiders certainly visited the area but, like the Ulaidh, did not build a town. Belfast was still no more than a crossing place when Anglo-Norman knights and freebooters swept into Ireland at the end of the twelfth century.

In 1177, one of these knights, John de Courcy, marched on Ulster with the intention of carving a fiefdom for himself. Ulster, one of Ireland's four provinces, consisted of the six north-eastern counties that nowadays comprise Northern Ireland as well as counties Cavan, Donegal and Monaghan. At this time, it was the most Gaelic province, ruled by fiercely independent chieftains. The north-east of Ireland now became a cockpit of conflict between the Gaelic lords and the Anglo-Normans, a conflict complicated by rivalries within both camps as well as the influx of Scottish marauders. Some time after de Courcy's incursion, the Anglo-Normans built a castle at the ford at Belfast. Much smaller and more vulnerable than the great keeps at Carrickfergus and Dundrum, it nevertheless occupied a strategic position and was attacked, demolished and rebuilt several times during the next three hundred years.

By the late sixteenth century, the Protestant Reformation and Catholic Counter-Reformation had cemented religious divisions within European Christendom. Under the Tudor monarchs England became Protestant, and the Church of England became the Established Church of the state. (Members of the Established Church were known as Anglicans, even in Ireland where the Established Church was called the Church of Ireland.) However, England was a small power and felt threatened by its larger Catholic neighbours, Spain and France: total control of Ireland was, therefore, deemed essential to secure England's western flank. Queen Elizabeth's commitment to Protestantism indicated England's determination to resist the encroaching influence of the two Catholic powers. In Ulster, the Gaelic chieftains and Old English nobles who had carved fiefdoms for themselves feared that their independence would be destroyed and they rebelled, led by the Earl of Tyrone, Hugh O'Neill, in 1595. After more years of bloody conflict, which brought victory for the Crown, the town of Belfast emerged.

2
SETTLEMENT IN
THE SEVENTEENTH CENTURY

One of the Crown's most successful soldiers in Ireland was Sir Arthur Chichester and for his services he was given, in a patent dated 5 November 1603, 'The Castle of Bealfaste or Belfast, with the Appurtenants and Hereditaments, Spiritual and Temporal, situate in the Lower Clandeboye, late in the possession or custody of Sir Ralph Lane Knt. deceased'. Chichester immediately rebuilt Belfast Castle and was further rewarded in 1605 when King James I appointed him Lord Deputy of Ireland. The new king had united the Crowns of England and Scotland and saw an opportunity to secure Ulster by installing trusted lieutenants who would undertake 'to inhabit the said territory with English or Scotchmen'.

A stream of Scots settlers began to cross the North Channel and most arrived in Clandeboye. Here they cleared woods and established a timber industry and farmed and practised their Presbyterianism without

Sir Arthur Chichester, 1563–1625 (artist unknown): appointed Lord Deputy of Ireland in 1605, he masterminded James I's Plantation in Ulster.
BELFAST HARBOUR COMMISSIONERS

interference from Anglican bishops. These were Lowland Scots, loyal to the Crown, and Chichester could do little but welcome those who travelled on to Belfast. After the Gaelic lords fled Ireland in 1607 in the so-called 'Flight of the Earls', the rest of Ulster was also opened to the Crown's plantation, or colonisation, plan. By 1611 the Plantation Commission reported favourably on progress in Belfast: 'The towne of Bealfast is plotted out in a good forme, wherein are many famelyes of English, Scotch, and some Manksmen already inhabitinge.'

In 1613 Chichester granted the small town a charter of incorporation as a borough. This meant it could elect two members to the Irish parliament: Belfast was a Protestant town and was trusted to return members whom Chichester could control in the interest of the Crown and his fellow nobles. The charter also granted limited local self-government, and here too the Chichester family held sway. Belfast's Sovereign (an office equivalent to mayor) was chosen by the twelve free burgesses from a shortlist of three drawn up by the head of the Chichester family. Presbyterians were excluded. The Chichesters controlled not only local lawmaking but also commerce, and over the next thirty years they benefited financially from changes to customs duties and by leasing land to the other landlords.

The overbearing control exercised by the Chichesters in part reflected the Anglican gentry's lingering suspicions of the mainly Presbyterian settlers. Efforts were made to enforce Anglican doctrine and all Scots in Ulster were required to take the 'Black Oath' of loyalty to the Crown. Religious, political and socio-economic tensions in and around Belfast between the Anglican elite and Presbyterian artisans, farmers and labourers were further complicated by the position of Catholics in the rest of Ulster.

Ulster Catholics, had been deprived of their most fertile lands and virtually all political influence, and in 1641 they again rose in rebellion. Belfast was never threatened directly, as the rebels were halted at Lisburn, but a rampart was erected to guard against future attack. General Robert Monro's Scots army provided welcome relief for Colonel Chichester in April 1642, but only months later they found themselves on opposite sides as civil war broke out in England, with the Chichesters supporting the Crown and Monro supporting Parliamentary forces. Only common fear of the Catholic Irish prevented open conflict.

When Chichester attempted to stop the Scots administering the Covenant to extirpate 'Popery, Prelacy, and Heresy', Monro captured a momentarily unguarded Belfast. Presbyterian fervour was soon checked, however. In June 1646, the Irish army of Owen Roe O'Neill routed Monro's army in Tyrone and Belfast gained a strategic importance second only to Dublin. A few months later, Monro's relations with English Parliamentarians, by now triumphant against the Crown, broke down. When Parliamentary Commissioners sailed into Belfast Lough in November 1646, Monro refused to hand over the town to them, and his nephew led a Scottish army to fight Parliamentary forces in England. Belfast surrendered to Colonel Monck's Parliamentary army in 1648 following Monro's capture at Carrickfergus but when Monck returned to England, Monro reoccupied the town in the name of the Crown. The Belfast Presbytery denounced parliament for opposing the Covenant and supporting religious toleration. John Milton wrote a blistering philosophical counter, but the arrival of Cromwell's army in Ireland had a more profound effect.

Colonel Robert Venables had responsibility for subduing Ulster, and by 1649 his army had reached Lisburn. From there he marched to Belfast and besieged the town for four days until the inhabitants yielded – this was the only siege in Belfast's history. For the next ten years the Commonwealth governed Ireland: Catholic landowners suffered the most sweeping confiscations in the country's history while Belfast in contrast, as an almost exclusively Protestant town, was relatively well treated. The Presbyterian Scots remained suspect as they had transferred their loyalties to the Crown, but as valuable allies against future Catholic rebellion they were not unduly harried.

Possession of Belfast had been important to all sides in the various wars but it suffered little as a town. Cromwell's iron rule provided a period of peace in which trade recovered, and on the eve of the restoration of the monarchy in 1660 the value of Belfast's seaborne trade was more than six times that of Carrickfergus. Belfast's citizens, Scots and English alike, were royalist in sympathy, and when General Monck returned to the town, this time at the head of the king's army, they gave him a warm welcome:

> Advance George Monck & Monck St George shall be
> Englands Restorer to Its Liberty
> Scotlands Protector Irelands President
> Reducing all to a ffree Parliam^t
> And if thou dost intend the other thinge
> Goe on and all shall Crye God save y^e Kinge.

The Restoration allowed the Chichesters, in the shape of Sir Arthur Chichester, 1st Earl of Donegall, to

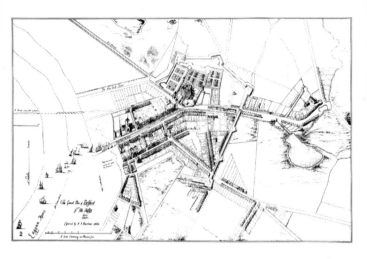

A ground plan of Belfast in 1685. This attractive nineteenth-century copy is somewhat confusing because South, contrary to all convention, is at the top of the plan.
LINEN HALL LIBRARY

regain control of Belfast. Ireland's economy prospered and nowhere more so than in Belfast which became Ulster's principal port for exporting agricultural surplus. Beef, butter, hides, tallow and corn were exported to France, Spain and the American colonies, which sent fruit, wine, delicacies and tobacco in return. In spite of this increased wealth, with a population of around one thousand Belfast remained a relatively small town. It had only two prominent buildings, the parish church and castle, and five main streets, High Street, Bridge Street, Waring Street, North Street and Skipper Street. The town's main street, High Street, followed the Farset river from the castle down to a dock. Further upstream, the Farset powered the town's cornmill (at the present Divis Street, adjacent to Millfield). Both established English families, such as the Warings, and recently arrived Scots, such as George Macartney, developed successful production and export businesses in tanning, sugar refining, corn and wool. They had little influence on town government, however, and Belfast's burgeoning middle class clearly resented the negligence and indolence of Chichester's creature, the Corporation. Although those of the richest merchants who were not Presbyterians, such as Macartney, did reach high office in the Corporation, they could not exercise control. The Irish parliament supported the Chichesters by ignoring a plea from Belfast's leading citizens to restructure the Corporation and make it more representative and responsive to the town's needs.

A more dramatic challenge to the Anglican elite's monopoly of power in Ireland came with the accession of James II, a Catholic king, in 1685. All Irish corporations were given new charters in 1688. In Belfast the number of burgesses was increased to thirty-five, about half of whom were local Presbyterians and half Catholic outsiders. Just three weeks later, in November 1688, the Protestant William of Orange landed in England to challenge for the throne. The citizens of Belfast responded by sending a pledge of allegiance to William.

Protected only by its rampart, Belfast was unable to resist the army of King James, which had defeated Ulster Protestant forces at Dromore in March 1689. While Derry kept its gates resolutely closed, Belfast's Sovereign, Thomas Pottinger, opened the town gates and surrendered, thus saving Belfast from assault and certain destruction. James's army showed restraint, but many citizens had already fled to Scotland. The arrival of the Williamite commander Schomberg with an army at Ballyholme Bay in August 1689 forced the Jacobite army to withdraw from Belfast and the town's old charter was soon restored. When William entered

Belfast in June 1690

> there were abundance to meet him at the North Gate,
> where he was received by the Sovereign and Burgesses
> in their formalities, a guard of Foot Guards, and a general
> continued shout from thence to the Castle of – God Bless
> our Protestant King, God Bless King William.

The citizens presented an address:

> Greatest of Kings, conquer what is your own,
> And add poor Ireland to sweet England's crown,
> Pull the stiff neck of every Papist down,
> Let captives free, who on the willow trees
> Hang useless harps that tuned such songs as these.

The bonfires that burned in the streets of Belfast in welcome were repeated annually thereafter and became a symbol of Protestant deliverance. William's eventual victory and accession to the throne inaugurated the most peaceful century in Belfast's history.

3
DEVELOPMENT IN
THE EIGHTEENTH CENTURY

William had promised the loyal Presbyterians of Belfast that they would 'enjoy their liberties and possessions under a just and equal government'. Until his death in 1702, Presbyterians seem to have retained control of the Corporation, whilst Presbyterian clergy throughout Ulster received the *regium donum*, an annual payment of £1,200. Queen Anne's accession to the throne brought the High Church Tories to power at Westminster, however, and the favourable treatment of Presbyterians ended abruptly. Until then, the Anglican gentry who dominated both the Westminster and Dublin parliaments had concentrated on restricting the power of the Catholic nobility through a range of Penal Laws; further extensive confiscations left all but 14 per cent of the land of Ireland in Protestant hands. The extension of the Penal Code in 1704 placed restrictions not only on Catholics but also on Presbyterians. Under the Test and Corporation Act all office holders under the Crown were required to take the sacrament in the Established Church. One of Belfast's two MPs, the Sovereign and eight burgesses, who all were Presbyterians, had to resign their offices. Belfast had a population of about 2,000, a majority of whom were Presbyterians, but the Penal Laws ensured that they would have no say in the running of the town's affairs.

Dr William Tisdall, Vicar of Belfast, was one of the most intolerant High Church Anglicans in Ireland. He shared the view of his close friend Jonathan Swift that Presbyterians were more to be feared than the Catholics, and he was instrumental in having the *regium donum* discontinued. This assault drew a firm response. Tisdall wanted to collect 'house-money' in Belfast to improve his income, and when this plan was blocked he brought a suit against the Corporation. Citizens of all denominations contributed to a fund to oppose him in court and his suit failed. James Blow, a Scots Presbyterian who printed the first Bible in Ireland at his Belfast press, defied Tisdall's efforts to impose censorship on the town by means of seizures of publications: Blow secretly reprinted a range of outlawed pamphlets.

Tisdall was supported by Lady Donegall, who in 1707 persuaded the Irish parliament that Belfast's Sovereign, Macartney, had been evading the Test and Corporation Act. Macartney was cleared, but High Church zeal was so intense that in 1713 eighty Belfast Anglicans signed a declaration in favour of toleration of their Presbyterian neighbours who stood accused of unfair trading. Similar support had been shown towards the town's small Catholic population. The Protestant Leslie family and Macartney protected Catholic clergy and their unofficial ceremonies. Catholics worshipped at Friar's Bush, where open-air Mass was celebrated on an oak table in a sandpit, and the town's tradesmen welcomed Catholic custom.

The Donegall family's continued power over Belfast not only created political and religious tensions but also made the town's development reliant upon the sagacity and commitment of the earl of the day. In 1706 the 3rd Earl was killed and his weak-willed young nephew, Arthur Chichester, succeeded him as the 4th Earl of Donegall. Two years later Belfast Castle burned down, the flames killing three of the 4th Earl's sisters. The family had lost its principal home, and its commitment to the town waned. Henceforth the Chichesters were

High Street, Belfast, in the 18th Century by J. W. Carey (1917): the painting
shows the parish church of Belfast, on the site where St George's Church was
built in 1816, with the Farset river running down the centre of the street.
BELFAST HARBOUR COMMISSIONERS

negligent, absentee landlords. The consequence for
Belfast was economic and infrastructural stagnation.

Development of the town was stifled above all by
short leases and tenancies that carried no obligation to
initiate improvements. Merchants threatened to 'leave
the town and settle in Newry or Lisburn' and in 1752
they pressed for an act of parliament granting long leases
'to promote or encourage the Rebuilding of the said
Town'. The promoters stated:

> The town of Belfast belongs to, and is the sole property of
> the Earl of Donegall, but as most of the Leases granted by
> the ancestors of the said Earl are now near expiring the
> Houses have been suffered to go out of repair, and so very
> old, ruinous, and unfit for habitation that it is become
> necessary for the Preservation and Support of the Trade
> of the Town and for preventing the Inhabitants from
> quitting and deserting the same, that the said Houses
> should be rebuilt.

Their petition to parliament was successful but the 4th
Earl of Donegall refused to act. It was not until the 5th

Earl succeeded his uncle in 1757 that new, longer leases, often covering the duration of three named lives, were issued. The price for such leases was higher rents and a commitment to make specified improvements. The town was carefully surveyed and penalties were fixed for tenants who dirtied the streets. A major rebuilding programme was soon under way. New building standards were set: in Castle Place houses had to be 28 feet high, in Castle Lane 15 feet; the cabins in Peter's Hill were to be 10 feet high. Important tenants were required to undertake major projects: Thomas Greg, for example, had to build a mortared quay wall 320 feet in length and to erect a drawbridge across the east end of the dock. Donegall's agent, John Gordon, recorded in 1757 that 'The Brick Grounds about the Town are most part run out and Brick will be much wanted.' New brickworks were established in what is now Sandy Row. In the first half of the century Belfast's growth had been almost imperceptible, but now it began to expand, rising from 8,500 in 1757 to 20,000 by 1800.

The increasing prosperity enjoyed by the Belfast gentry and middle classes was not experienced by the labouring classes. In July 1756 Macartney wrote, 'All Order and Government here are now at an end': crowds of people, unable to buy what little grain was for sale in the town, were seizing sacks of meal and forcing shopkeepers to sell bread at below market price. Stability did not return until a good autumn harvest had been garnered in. But the town's propertied leaders had been frightened: they responded by rounding up the mob's ringleaders and by initiating a scheme for the relief of the poor.

Unlike England, Ireland had no Poor Law system, and neither the Donegall family nor the Corporation had provided an alternative. The philanthropists therefore developed a scheme through the Belfast Charitable Society, which had been established in 1752. However, the original ambition of raising £50,000 was quickly dashed: by 1767 only £7,592 had been raised. This money would have been best spent on outdoor relief – whereby food and clothing was given to the poor in their own homes. However, contemporary moral and political philosophy deemed the healthy poor to be idle and undeserving, and the Poor House, where those seeking assistance were required to live, was built instead. Now called Clifton House, Belfast's unpretentious yet imposing Poor House is one of the finest buildings in Belfast today.

That same year Lord Donegall re-leased large parts of his property. Farms and land were re-let at old rents, which were attractively low, plus a heavy 'fine'. These fines were large one-off payments intended to allow the 5th Earl to raise the quick capital needed to defray the family debt and pay for his extravagant lifestyle. Many tenants could not pay these fines and were evicted, whilst others found that Belfast merchants had bid over their heads for the leases of whole townlands. William Grey, for example, rented the half-townland of Ballyclaverty for £57 10s. 0d. but paid a fine of £400; Dr Haliday leased Ballyduff for £120 10s. 0d. and a £500 fine; and Robert Wallace obtained a lease for Ballymurphy at a rent of £100 2s. 0d. and a fine of £170. These middlemen, described by the agricultural improver Arthur Young as 'the most oppressive species of tyrant that ever lent assistance to the destruction of a nation', acted as speculators and put up rents when subletting. Poor tenants who defaulted on their rents were ejected and replaced by solvent tenants.

When, in 1770, the Upton family evicted tenants on their Templepatrick estate and installed two of the Belfast speculators, Thomas Greg and Waddell Cunningham, a crisis erupted. Angry local farmers gathered at Templepatrick Meeting House and marched on Belfast. Sympathisers joined the mob *en route* and by the time it reached the Shore Road in north Belfast they numbered 1,200. Calling themselves the 'Hearts of Steel' they demanded the release of David Douglas, who was being held for maiming cattle belonging to Greg. The Sovereign, Stewart Banks, closed the north gate of the town and withdrew to the Barrack with twenty-five armed men. When the mob discovered this

> they fired many shots at the gate and over the wall, but failing of the desired effect, a party proceeded to the house of Waddell Cunningham, broke it open, and were in the act of destroying the furniture when Dr Haliday, ... dreading lest the town might be destroyed, mingled with the crowd. ... After expostulating with them in vain he was taken prisoner by them and sworn, that he would immediately repair to the Barrack and procure the release of the prisoner. ... The Doctor had just reached the Barrack on this embassy, passing through an immense multitude consisting of the people from the country intermixed with those of the town, when the gate was thrown open by the military, who fired upon the assailants, killed five persons and wounded nine others.

Cunningham's house had caught fire, and Banks felt he had no choice but to hand over the prisoner to prevent the destruction of Belfast. Disturbances continued throughout 1771 and 1772, prompting the landlords to ask the Lord Lieutenant, Townshend, for troops. These were sent reluctantly, Townshend lamenting that such action would 'compel wretched tenants to go to

America, or any other part of the world where they can receive that reward which is honestly due to their labour'.

Throughout the seventeenth century, Lowland Scots had poured into Ulster. By the close of Queen Anne's reign in 1714 there were approximately 200,000 Presbyterians in the province out of a total population of around 600,000. At this point immigration virtually ceased, and for the next sixty years there was a spectacular outpouring of so-called 'Scotch-Irish' to America, 'the Land of Promise'. By the middle of the eighteenth century it was reckoned that 12,000 were leaving Ulster every year. Although the most distressed areas were in western Ulster, Belfast was the most important port of departure; around 143 emigrant vessels sailed from the town between 1750 and 1775.

Four years before the Hearts of Steel riots, the *Belfast News-Letter* was encouraging its readers to sail to Nova Scotia and embrace 'a favourable opportunity . . . which cannot fail to give freedom, peace and plenty'. Many Ulster Protestants, mindful that they had done so much to defeat the Irish Jacobites, deeply resented the commercial restrictions imposed on Ireland by Westminster to protect the mother country's interests. Dr Boulter of Belfast lamented that the 'contagious distemper' of emigration 'affects only Protestants and reigns chiefly in the north, which is the seat of our linen manufacture'.

The Ulster linen industry had developed rapidly in the eighteenth century but it was a cottage industry reliant upon buoyant export markets. The small farmers and rural labourers who worked in linen to augment their income from agriculture were thus vulnerable to any prolonged depression in international trade – such as occurred in the 1770s. Earnings from linen rose by about 20 per cent between 1710 and 1770, but the increase was not enough to compensate for the escalation in rents, which quintupled in many areas during the same period. Population growth had increased the demands on land, and for those unable to compete emigration was an attractive option. The gulf between middle-class Belfast and the Belfast of the labouring masses who remained behind was apparent to one traveller in 1780:

> ... in my entrance into Belfast I was vastly surprized and hurt to see a long string of falling cabins and tattered houses, all tumbling down with a horrid aspect, and the seeming prelude to a pitiful village which was my idea of Belfast, untill I got pretty far into the town when I found my error, for indeed with some trifling improvements it might be made to vie with any town in Ireland save Dublin and Cork.

The rebuilding programme initiated in the 1750s had transformed Belfast into Ireland's 'third commercial

High Street, 1786: a late-nineteenth-century copy of a contemporary engraving. The Donegall Arms (left foreground) was the principal hotel of the time. The dial-plate of the Market House clock (right foreground) fell and severely injured a man earlier in the century.
ULSTER MUSEUM

town'. The architect Roger Mulholland planned and built many fine houses for the gentry and merchants in and around the town's main thoroughfares, Castle Street and High Street. One of his most enduring successes was the 1st Presbyterian Church in Rosemary Street, built in 1783, which the preacher John Wesley described as 'the completest place of worship I have ever seen'. For the Anglicans Lord Donegall paid for the erection of St Anne's parish church in 1776 (this was pulled down in 1900 to make way for St Anne's Cathedral). Near Peter's Hill in the north of the town, now becoming a fashionable area, 'Mr Ryder's New Theatre in Mill Gate opened in 1770, augmenting the Vaults playhouse in Ann Street. Two years later, one traveller described the town centre:

> The houses are well built with brick and slated, with the streets pretty wide; the pavement is bad in some places, but not in general. Were conduits of water run through them, which I think might be effected at an easy expense, it would take off the dirt which unavoidably gathers, and this with shameful heaps in many streets, must be a very great nuisance to the inhabitants. . . . A New Town Hall is now building; it is a gift of the Lord and on a handsome design, but scarcely long enough for its height. I hear the underpart is to serve for an Exchange, and the upper part for an Assembly Room . . .

The Exchange had been built in 1769 and the Assembly Rooms were completed in 1777. Nearby was the Stone Bridge – the town's business centre – where ships discharged their cargoes at the quays, the post office, and the *Belfast News-Letter* offices. But, if private enterprise was flourishing, the 'shameful heaps' of filth remained a public problem. The Farset still flowed uncovered through High Street (it was covered in stages from the 1770s onwards) and, according to a traveller in 1780, 'piles of dunghills made up through the middle of the whole town from one end to the other'.

Belfast did not play a leading part in the development of the linen industry, which had become Ireland's second most valuable export – worth nearly £1.5 million a year by the 1760s, just behind provisions. Belfast was on the edge of Ulster's main linen production area, however, being the northern point of the triangle formed with Armagh and Dungannon and including the principal linen markets, namely Lurgan, Armagh and Lisburn. In the early eighteenth century most of Ulster's linen was sold in Dublin, to be taken subsequently for sale in London, but in 1782 there was a bitter dispute over trade regulations between the leading Ulster drapers and the Dublin merchants. As a result, the drapers decided to bypass Dublin and set up their own linen halls.

'Brown' or unbleached linen had been sold in Belfast since the 1740s, at the Brown Linen Hall built by Lord Donegall, but 'white', bleached linen had faced restric-

South of the White Linen Hall (left centre) and Joy's mill dam (right centre), Belfast was still essentially rural: *Belfast*, an engraving by John Nixon, published in 1793.

tive duties. When Westminster removed these duties in 1779–80, Irish linen was granted privileged access to British markets and Belfast was given an incentive to oversee its own sales. Lord Donegall gave land for a white linen hall to be built for that purpose on the site where the City Hall now stands, and the first stone was laid in April 1783. The White Linen Hall was a plain, quadrangular building and for many years much of the south side remained unfinished. Part of the reason for this was the success of men such as Arthur Young, James Ferguson, John Wolfenden and William Sinclair, who invested capital and expertise in making Belfast a centre for the bleaching of linen and became so prosperous that they were able to deal directly with the British market, thus undermining the function of the White Linen Hall.

Linen was of growing importance but as in Britain it was cotton that provided Belfast with its first major industrial development. In July 1776 the *Belfast News-Letter* advertised the visit of an English businessman, Nicholas Grimshaw, who was to talk about the new techniques of mass production, such as Arkwright's water-frame and carding machine, that were revolutionising the economy of northern England. When Robert Joy, a Belfast entrepreneur and philanthropist, toured Britain the following year seeking ideas to provide employment for Poor House inmates, he 'conceived the scheme of introducing ... the most intricate Branches of the Cotton Manufacture which had proved unfailing sources of Industry and Opulence to our sister country'. Upon returning to Belfast he formed a partnership with his brother Henry, the watchmaker Thomas McCabe and John McCracken. They built a mill in Francis Street employing ninety workers, many of them children from the Poor House, and used machinery driven by a sixteen-horsepower water wheel 'to spin twist by water, in the manner of Richard Arkwright'. The government helped by providing funding and by enacting a protective duty on cotton in 1794.

Other mills soon sprang up, including Thomas Hazlett's in Waring Street and Messrs Stevensons' at Springfield, where the first steam engine was employed. In 1782 there were only 25 spinning jennies in Belfast but by 1791 there were 229. The machine-spun thread was sent to handloom weavers who worked in their own homes but were paid by the employers; by 1791 there were 522 looms weaving cotton in Belfast. Giving evidence to the House of Commons in 1800, Grimshaw stated that within a ten-mile radius of Belfast £192,000 was invested in the cotton industry, providing work for 13,500 people. The first industrial revolution had arrived in Ireland, and it was in Belfast that it took the firmest hold.

The developments initiated by Belfast's middle class extended to education. The Donegall family expected residents to use the school built by the 1st Earl in 1666, but by the 1750s it was clear that many prominent families were not prepared to do so. In 1754 David Manson, perhaps the most progressive educationalist in Ireland, advertised an 'Evening School' at his home in Clugston's Entry. Using capital from his successful brewing business, he established a school in High Street in 1760 and another in Donegall Street in 1768. Presbyterians led by Dr William Bruce built the Belfast Academy (known today as Belfast Royal Academy) in 1786. Whilst the Belfast Academy served only boys and relied upon strict discipline, Manson promised to teach both boys and girls 'to spell, read, and understand the English Tongue without the discipline of the Rod'.

The values of the Enlightenment were at last filtering into Belfast.

When American colonists rose in rebellion against George III in 1775, the sympathy of the Protestants of Belfast was with them. As the Reverend W. S. Dickson put it: 'There is scarcely a Protestant family of the middle classes amongst us who does not reckon kindred with the inhabitants of that extensive continent.' Lord Newhaven told the Westminster parliament that Washington was able to 'oppose our armies with our own Irish subjects, whom our narrow policy has driven from their country'. Lord Harcourt reported to Dublin Castle that the Ulster Presbyterians were Americans 'in their hearts'. On 4 November 1775 a great meeting of 'the Merchants, Traders, and other principal Inhabitants of the Town of Belfast' agreed to send an address to George III, 'humbly and fervently imploring your Majesty to sheath the sword of civil war'.

The entry of France on the side of the colonists in 1778 put the citizens of Belfast in a quandary: they sympathised with the Americans but the French, who had briefly captured Carrickfergus eighteen years before, were traditional enemies of Protestant liberties. Some Belfast men made up their minds immediately and on St Patrick's Day 1778 formed the 1st Belfast Volunteer Company to protect against French invasion. A month later, a successful raid on Belfast Lough by the American naval commander John Paul Jones in his ship *Ranger* highlighted the weakness of British forces in Ireland and Belfast's vulnerability to invasion and persuaded the ambivalent to act. Belfast Protestants had faced similar threats during the Jacobite rebellions of 1715 and 1745 and had formed Volunteer companies to protect the town. Survivors of the 1745 scare met in the

Donegall Arms Hotel on 16 April 1778 and formed a second Volunteer company. The volunteers were soon organised in military form, with Irish-made uniforms, a band and the Reverend Bryson as Presbyterian chaplain.

During 1779, the government's position in Ireland grew increasingly desperate. Trade was depressed, which resulted in widespread distress, and only an advance of £50,000 from the Bank of England saved the Irish Treasury from bankruptcy. Without surplus capital, the Dublin parliament could not afford to raise a militia to act as a temporary replacement for the regular troops that had been sent to America to aid the hard-pressed Crown forces. The government had no choice but to arm the Volunteers, whose numbers throughout Ireland grew to around 45,000. From this strong position, and with the support of the Patriot group in the Irish parliament, the Volunteers pressed for political reform.

Ireland's constitutional position resembled that of some of the American colonies that were now in revolt. The Irish parliament was an exclusive club for the landed gentry but its powers were emasculated by Westminster, which not only controlled foreign affairs but could also alter or suppress bills passed by the Irish parliament. It also appointed the Irish executive that administered Ireland from Dublin Castle. Patriot MPs, led by Henry Grattan and Henry Flood, and the Volunteers, led by their commander Lord Charlemont, wanted the Irish parliament to have legislative independence and thus more control over Irish affairs. Many Patriots were uncomfortable, however, with the Volunteers' militarism. Westminster stood firm.

The Volunteers' response to the government was

strongest in Belfast, where three days of military manoeuvres and reviews were held in July 1780. A *Belfast News-Letter* reporter observed:

> It is difficult to say which called most for admiration, the spectacle, or the spectators? Three thousand men in arms, steady, uniform, obedient, *breathing the spirit of loyalty and liberty!* or thirty thousand spectators, building their hopes of peace and security on the skill and activity displayed by their neighbours, friends, and children, in the field.

Resolutions carried by the Belfast men were among the most fiery in the country: 'If the resolute defence of national rights and liberties be sedition we will not then scruple to denominate the Volunteers of Ireland traitors.' The Volunteers' review was repeated the following July with approximately 100,000 spectators in attendance. British defeat in America, at Yorktown in October 1781, weakened the government and strengthened the reformers' position. In early 1782 the Tory government at Westminster fell and the new Whig ministry immediately granted the demand for legislative independence.

Westminster could no longer emasculate laws passed by the Dublin parliament but it still appointed the Irish executive, thereby retaining great influence over Irish affairs. Moreover, the Irish parliament remained the preserve of the Anglican landed gentry, or, as they were to be commonly dubbed, the Protestant Ascendancy. Catholics were forbidden to vote or to sit in parliament, whilst Nonconformists such as the Presbyterians who dominated Belfast felt they were not represented:

> ... although the borough of Belfast sends two Members to [the Dublin] Parliament, yet those members are returned (under the immediate direction of a noble peer)

by five or six Burgesses, in the appointment of whom your Petitioners have no share, and therefore the Members cannot in *any* sense, be deemed the Representatives of your Petitioners.

Delegates of thirty-nine corps reviewed in Belfast in June 1783 resolved:

That at an era so honourable to the spirit, wisdom, and loyalty of Ireland, A MORE EQUAL REPRESENTATION of the People in Parliament deserves the deliberate attention of every Irishman.

But this was not a call for universal suffrage. The Belfast delegates at the Volunteer convention in Dublin in the winter of 1783–84 represented the town's aspiring middle class. This respectability undermined the Volunteers' military threat and allowed the Irish parliament to call their bluff. Barry Yelverton, the Attorney General, protested that 'we sit not here to register the edicts of another assembly or to receive propositions at the point of a bayonet'. The Belfast delegates were disappointed not only by the Dublin parliament's reaction but also because they had failed to convince the Volunteer convention that Catholics should be included in the campaign for political reform.

No Protestants in Ireland called more vociferously for Catholic emancipation than the Belfast Volunteers. Across the island, Protestants were a minority fearing Catholic insurrection and French invasion. In Ulster, Protestants and Catholics were roughly equal in number but this did nothing to reduce tensions. Ancient feuds over land remained unresolved and in areas where the linen industry had developed, like north Armagh, new rivalries developed for weaving work. Belfast, however, was in the most Protestant corner of Ireland where Catholics were too poor and too few in number to pose a threat. The Presbyterian middle class viewed the continued domination of Belfast's Corporation and parliamentary representation by the Chichester family as a greater problem. Their cultivation of progressive ideas – in Manson's schools, in the pages of the *Belfast News-Letter*, and at Glasgow and Edinburgh universities – provided the intellectual framework for the political challenge presented by the Volunteers.

The Belfast Volunteers resolved to enrol Catholics in May 1784, inviting 'to our ranks, persons of *every* religious persuasion'. On 30 May the two Belfast companies 'paraded in full dress, and marched to MASS, where a sermon was preached by the Rev Mr O'Donnell and a handsome collection made to aid in defraying the expense of erecting the new Mass-house. – Great numbers of the other Protestant inhabitants also attended.' The £84 collected by Belfast Protestants enabled St Mary's Chapel to be built (at a total cost of £170). Belfast's Catholic population had grown from 556 in 1757 to about 1,000 in the 1780s but Catholics had had no official place of worship until in 1782 a seventy-one-year lease was taken on a house in Crooked Lane (now Chapel Lane). The erection of St Mary's Chapel and Father O'Donnell's public letter of thanks to the Volunteers led the *Belfast News-Letter* to ask, 'Whilst such perfect concord distinguishes the Irish nation, what moderate demand founded in truth and right can it ever make that can be long refused?'

But the campaign for parliamentary reform and Catholic emancipation failed; one MP described Belfast as a nest of traitors and rebels. Seeking to avoid a confrontation with Dublin Castle, Lord Charlemont persuaded the bulk of the Volunteers to show restraint.

The reform movement slowly lost momentum. Dr William Drennan, a leading radical, wrote in March 1785: 'I was in Belfast lately for a day and among all the friends of Reform of all Churches. Zeal is entirely sunk to the lower classes, and Reform is now but seldom the topic of conversation in any genteel society.' Drennan was already sketching a plan for a secret conspiracy, but it was not until the revolution in France in 1789 that he was able to realise his dream.

Throughout the summer of 1789, the *Belfast News-Letter* provided its eager audience with detailed reports of the revolution. Henry Joy wrote, 'the friends of Liberty once more turned their undivided attention to the salutory measure of reform'. Ever eager to channel such zeal into moderate enterprise, Charlemont encouraged Dr Haliday to establish a branch of the Irish Whig Club in Belfast in February 1790. This provided a support mechanism for parliamentary candidates who supported reform, such as John O'Neill and Henry Rowley who won the County Antrim election in June. The Northern Whig Club reached the peak of its influence in 1791 when on 14 July it celebrated in Belfast the second anniversary of the fall of the Bastille. Belfast Volunteers, watched by thousands, marched from the Exchange down High Street. At the White Linen Hall they resolved to send a declaration of appreciation to the people of France. It concluded:

As IRISHMEN, we too have a country, and we hold it very dear – so dear to us its *Interest*, that we wish all *Civil and Religious Intolerance* annihilated in this land. . . .

Go on then – Great and Gallant People! – to practise the sublime philosophy of your legislation . . . and not by conquest, but by the omnipotence of reason, to convert and liberate the World . . .

In August 1791, addresses of thanks from Nantes and Bordeaux were printed in the *Courier de l'Europe*. The Protestant middle class seemed unanimous in its support for reform, yet there were already signs of the irrevocable split that would cause some to draw back and drive others to revolution.

A list of Belfast reformers would be, in effect, a roll-call of almost all the persons of property in the town. Many were intimate friends and business colleagues; indeed, many were related to one another. All were Protestants. The brothers Henry and Robert Joy were editors of the *Belfast News-Letter* and enthusiastic Volunteers. Their sister Ann had married Captain John McCracken and the couple's sons – Francis, William, Henry Joy and John – and daughters – Rose Ann, Margaret and Mary Ann – were all avid reformers. As a revolutionary, social reformer and advocate of women's rights, Mary Ann is perhaps the town's most famous woman. Henry Joy McCracken and fellow merchants such as Thomas McCabe, Samuel Neilson, Robert and William Simms, Robert Getty and Thomas Sinclair met with Dr Haliday, Thomas Greg and Waddell Cunningham at Mrs McTier's 'coteries' to discuss politics. These radicals initially belonged to no group, but under the direction of Dr William Drennan, who was Mrs McTier's brother, they were to become the United Irishmen.

'How does your Whig Club?' Drennan asked Sam McTier in 1791. He believed that the reform movement was too respectable and moderate and that his scheme, first formulated in 1784, to form a society 'as secret as the Free-masons ... to put into execution plans for the complete liberation of the country', was the only alternative. He composed for McTier a proposal for 'a benevolent conspiracy – a plot for the people – no Whig Club – no party title – the Brotherhood its name – the Rights of Man and the Greatest Happiness of the Greatest Number its end – its general end Real Independence to Ireland, and Republicanism its particular purpose'. McTier put this scheme to the Belfast reformers and on 1 April 1791 an organising committee met in Peggy Barclay's tavern in Crown Entry, off High Street. There they resolved 'to form ourselves into an association to unite all Irishmen to pledge ourselves to our country, and by that cordial union maintain that balance of patriotism so essential for the restoration and preservation of our liberty, and the revival of our trade – Signed: Samuel Neilson, John Robb, Alexander Lowry, Thomas McCabe, and Henry Joy McCracken.'

Wolfe Tone, a Dublin Protestant who had written *An Argument on Behalf of the Catholics of Ireland*, was invited to join and in October he arrived in Belfast. There he met the secret committee, helped to draft a declaration of their aims, and suggested a name, the Society of United Irishmen. However, the discovery of Drennan's 'plot for the people' by government authorities meant that a conspiracy was out of the question. On 21 October 1791 the society was officially launched in public, its aim being to achieve 'a cordial union among all the people of Ireland' and 'a complete and radical reform of the representation of the people of Ireland of every religious persuasion'. The first great revival of Irish traditional music, at the Belfast Harp Festival held in July 1792, was organised by the group with such national unity in mind. The power of public opinion, its members hoped, would frighten the Dublin parliament into conceding reform and would preclude the need for revolution.

But the reform movement was now deeply divided. Many moderates in Belfast saw the United Irishmen's brinkmanship strategy as too extreme and thus drew back. For Tone, however, the strategy was too slow. Rather than organise a harp festival to 'Strum and be hanged', Tone wanted the United Irishmen to commit themselves to revolution.

In April 1792 revolutionary France declared war on her neighbours and in September the mob broke into the Paris jails and mutilated and murdered the prisoners. Mrs McTier wrote, 'I am turned, quite turned, against the French.' In January 1793 Louis XVI was executed and by February Britain was at war with France. The government viewed the Belfast radicals, now spreading the United Irish message through the pages of the *Northern Star* newspaper, as little better than traitors. In March 1793 the Lord Lieutenant suppressed the Belfast Volunteers, to the dismay of moderates and radicals alike. Soldiers ran amok in the town, Sam McTier recording that their commander, Colonel French, 'swore by God if there was one gun fired from any Window at any of his people he would immediately burn the Town'. The *Northern Star* was prosecuted in 1792, 1793 and 1794, forcing one of the owners, Samuel Neilson, to mortgage his woollen warehouse business to defray the legal costs.

In an attempt to stop Catholic men of property joining Presbyterian radicals, Westminster forced the Irish parliament to grant Catholics the vote in 1793. Instead of contenting the reformers, however, this convinced them that full Catholic emancipation was imminent. It was not, and in 1795, Lord Fitzwilliam was forced to resign as Lord Lieutenant because he had supported a campaign to remove the last of the Penal Laws. On

4 March 1795 a town meeting of 'the inhabitants of Belfast' voted to hold a day of national mourning in response. With Westminster resolved on maintaining the Protestant Ascendancy and all hope of reform through constitutional activity seemingly gone, the prospect of a United Irish rebellion drew closer.

However, by 1795 the Protestant middle class was not united in zeal for Catholic emancipation, never mind revolution; the United Irish radicals were divided into those who rejected revolution and those, like Tone, who desired it. Dr James McDonnell, Dr William Bruce and Joy junior urged loyalty to the Crown and remained hopeful that a popular protest movement would push Dublin Castle into granting reform. They assumed that the people would follow them, yet none seem to have had Catholic friends and only Henry Joy McCracken seems to have had any close friends amongst the labouring classes. In contrast to their naïve optimism, Tone had been laying plans for a revolution that relied not upon the spontaneous action of the Irish masses but on the assistance of the French.

Henry Joy McCracken: in 1798 he led the United Irishmen at the Battle of Antrim and was subsequently hanged at Cornmarket.
ULSTER MUSEUM

Only family connections in high places prevented Wolfe Tone from being executed in 1795. Arrested for treasonable negotiations with a French spy, he was ordered into exile and in May 1795 he arrived in Belfast with his family in order to sail to America. United Irish colleagues provided hospitality, and on the summit of McArt's Fort, on Cave Hill high above the town, they made a solemn vow 'never to desist in our efforts until we have subverted the authority of England over our country and asserted her independence'. Meanwhile Belfast radicals had sown a crop of United Irish societies in north Down and south and central Antrim; there, the Antrim weaver Jemmy Hope wrote, 'The republican spirit, inherent in the principles of the Presbyterian community, kept resistance to arbitrary power still alive.'

In the autumn of 1795 these Protestant farmers and Belfast idealists gained unlikely allies. West of the River Bann the new ideas had made little progress; there, seventeenth-century hatred festered in the bitter rivalry to hold land close to the linen markets. Savage sectarian warfare reached a crescendo on 21 September 1795 when the Catholic Defenders were routed by the Protestant Peep o' Day Boys at the so-called Battle of the Diamond near Loughgall. The victors founded the Orange Order, whilst the Defenders, first in mid-Ulster and then throughout Leinster, joined the United Irish-men *en masse*. As Ireland drifted towards civil war, the government quickly enrolled Protestant and Catholic supporters into the yeomanry and militia.

The amateur preparations of the Belfast leaders of the United Irishmen were soon exposed by spies and informers. In September 1796 Samuel Neilson, Thomas Russell and Charles Teeling were arrested and the

Northern Star presses were destroyed. Henry Joy McCracken was arrested the following month and held in Dublin's Newgate prison. In December 1796 a French fleet, with Tone on board as a French army officer, was in Bantry Bay. Though foul weather prevented a landing, the British administration in Dublin Castle realised that its poorly trained militia men were no match for 14,000 French veterans. The suppression of the revolutionary north could no longer be postponed.

General Lake, Commander of the Northern District, declared in March 1797 that 'Belfast ought to be . . . punished most severely, as it is plain every act of sedition originates in this town'. Martial law was imposed and troops were unleashed on the town. The property of known radicals and the premises of the *Northern Star* were destroyed, suspects were arrested and held without trial (many of the leaders were held in the hulk *Postlethwaite* in the Pool of Garmoyle below Belfast); men were flogged in the streets. Lake reported, 'The flame is smothered but not extinguished.' The French émigré de Latocnaye observed, 'The people of this town, who were represented some time ago as about to rise, appear now in a sort of stupor hardly distinguishable from fear.' Government repression may have sparked the United Irish rising in Leinster, but in Belfast repression was highly successful. As Carlow and Kildare erupted in May 1798, there was no immediate response in the north.

By now released from prison, Henry Joy McCracken was the only United Irish leader in Belfast who joined the rising. Jemmy Hope recalled: 'When all our leaders deserted us, Henry Joy McCracken stood alone faithful to the last.' The second largest garrison in Ireland was

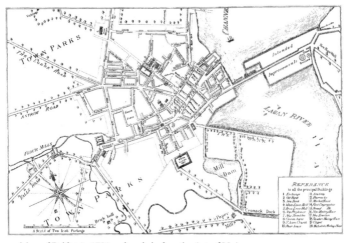

Map of Belfast in 1791, a decade before the Act of Union.
LINEN HALL LIBRARY

stationed in Belfast, so McCracken and Hope led their men towards Antrim instead. An uprising took place in Down also, but defeat was inevitable. The captured McCracken was taken to Belfast in July, tried, convicted and hanged at the corner of Cornmarket and High Street. Not only had the United Irish movement been destroyed but the noble ideal of the Belfast democrats – to achieve 'a cordial union among all the people of Ireland' – had been betrayed at Wexford. There, the United Irish were drawn mainly from the Catholic Defenders, and their rebellion had spiralled into a slaughter of local Protestants. Some Belfast radicals held on to the United Irish dream, refusing to inform on fellow conspirators and paying with their lives. Others, shocked by the reluctance of the masses to follow their lead and by the sectarian blood-letting at Wexford, resigned themselves to defeat.

In response to the rising the government proposed an Act of Union between Britain and Ireland. The Dublin

35

parliament was abolished and Irish MPs were elected to the Westminster parliament which became the sole legislative body for the United Kingdom of Great Britain and Ireland. In Belfast, no great passion either for or against was displayed. Only manufacturers, who feared that protective duties on cotton would be discontinued, and the Marquis of Donegall, who feared that the Protestant Ascendancy would be undermined, questioned the idea. The manufacturers received guarantees and the marquis died soon afterwards: his son and successor was reconciled to the Union by the offer of a command in the yeomanry. In the years ahead, however, the Union was to become the focus of fierce debate amongst the people of Belfast.

4
ECONOMIC GROWTH
AND POLITICAL CHANGE
1800–70

The war with France had a more immediate impact on Belfast than the Act of Union. A French blockade of British and Irish trade with Europe forced the new United Kingdom to feed, clothe and arm itself. This provided a stimulus to Belfast's industry and brought new investment. British demand for food increased and corn and meat prices rose, bringing greater prosperity to farmers, landlords and traders throughout Ireland, and it was in Ireland that most of Belfast's cotton was sold. As cotton carts rattled through Sandy Row to markets far off in the south and west, the skyline of Belfast was increasingly broken by mill chimneys.

An estimated £350,000 was invested in Belfast's

View of Belfast from Old Park hill, 1855, by Hugh Frazer. The large chimney in the centre of the painting is probably that of the Old Park Print Works, owned by William Girdwood and Company.
BELFAST HARBOUR COMMISSIONERS

cotton industry between 1800 and 1812. In what is now North Queen Street, the McCrum, Leppers and Co. mill behind the Artillery Barracks, measuring 200 feet in length and five storeys high, was for a time the largest in Ireland. This was surpassed in 1822 by Thomas Mulholland's new mill at Point Fields. Cotton was king in Belfast and Belfast was king of Irish cotton.

Cotton was a volatile business, however. Fortunes were made and lost with equal speed and the 2,000 or so workers employed in the industry faced sudden and periodic unemployment. An Anglo–American trade war in 1809 left the industry 'in a state of deepest depression', but in 1811 cotton wool worth £250,000 was processed into cloth worth around £1 million. The victory at Waterloo brought the wartime boom to an end, with prices tumbling in 1816 by about 30–40 per cent, but Belfast maintained a considerable cotton business.

In the boom years a factory cotton spinner had a relatively good income of about £2 7s. 0d. a week. Weavers, by comparison, had very low earnings, of between 12 and 15 shillings a week. Although most cotton weavers worked at home, few worked for themselves; instead they were employed directly by manufacturers and paid 'prices' or piece rates.

In times of depression manufacturers unhesitatingly cut 'prices'. Before 1824 weavers could not by law form 'combinations', or trade unions, but they did take collective action to try and prevent such wage reductions. In 1815 one Belfast employer, Francis Johnston, was 'sworn out of trade'; that is, weavers took an oath not to work for him. This action was followed by an unsuccessful bomb attack on Johnston's house. Three weavers were tried and hanged for this in Castle Street – these were the last public executions performed in Belfast.

By 1825 around one third of the weavers in the Belfast area were unemployed, whilst the remainder endured a grim life on below-subsistence wages. In depression years, weavers worked from 4 a.m. to midnight seven days a week for a wage of four shillings and sixpence. The *Belfast News-Letter* reported in 1830 that Ballymacarrett weavers were living on Indian meal unfit for cattle and looked like skeletons in consequence of overwork and lack of sleep.

The rapid growth of Ireland's population and the impoverishment of much of the countryside ultimately account for the weavers' distress. The labourers who poured into Belfast faster than work could be created for them pushed Belfast's total population from 20,000 in 1800 to over 70,000 by 1841. The burgeoning

Review of the Belfast Yeomanry by the Lord Lieutenant, the Earl of Hardwicke,
27 August 1804 by Thomas Robinson. The artist included a statue of Nelson in the painting in order to make it more saleable, though no such statue ever existed in Belfast. Those who appear in the painting include the Marquis of Donegall, Sir Edward May, Dr William Bruce and Henry Joy junior – an indication of the social standing of the town's middle class.
BELFAST HARBOUR COMMISSIONERS

population allowed employers to keep wages low and made it unnecessary for them to cut labour costs by installing power looms. Lancashire cotton products, woven by steam-powered looms and often finer in quality, captured Belfast's Irish markets after 1824, when Westminster removed tariffs between Britain and Ireland. Belfast cotton manufacturers had both the capital and expertise to modernise and compete, but by the 1830s they had decided that linen offered more profitable opportunities.

The businessmen, merchants and manufacturers of Belfast had been prising the Chichester family from its hold on the town even before the cotton boom years, but their growing prosperity after 1800 and the Chichesters' mounting difficulties accelerated this process. In the 1790s Lord Belfast had run up huge debts and in 1795 he secretly married the illegitimate daughter of Sir Edward May, creating both financial and legal problems for his family. When he became 2nd Marquis of Donegall in 1799 the family debts totalled over £200,000. As a result of restrictions imposed by previous settlements of the family inheritance, land could not be sold easily to raise capital. After years of delays while the courts decided that the Marquis's marriage was legal, an elaborate new settlement of the Donegall estates was made in 1822. Over 1,500 perpetual leases were sold for large sums in cash, fixing the old low rents for all time; about 600 of these leases were for properties in the Belfast area.

The Belfast middle class bought leases as they not only gave them additional security for borrowing but also conferred on them the prestige of being virtual landowners. Also, unlike in 1767, there were no regulations governing the leases. Purchasers could build or sublet as they wished, so the sale effectively opened the way for Belfast's expansion. The money allowed the Donegalls to build the mock-Tudor Ormeau House facing the Ravenhill Road, complete with pheasantry and 'race-course', and to indulge in the lifestyle of the gentry once again. Despite this, it was clear that the family's influence was waning.

In 1800, just before its extinction, the Irish parliament had enacted the Belfast Police Act. The act was almost a declaration that the Corporation still controlled by the Donegalls had failed to carry out its duties. Two police boards were set up: the Committee of Police elected annually by ratepayers to act as a supervising executive, and the Commission of Police, a body of twenty-one individuals elected for life and responsible not only for arresting suspects to be brought before a magistrate but also for paving, lighting, town cleaning, and providing a fire service and night watch. The night watch constables concentrated their efforts on patrolling the docks area where prostitution was rife. In the main, though, the Commission of Police endeavoured to clean up and regulate Belfast by imposing fines on polluters and by labelling streets and numbering houses as the town grew. The biggest project undertaken by the Commissioners and the Committee of Police was the construction of the gasworks on the Ormeau Road in 1821–23 to supply Belfast with gas lighting at a cost of £40,000.

Belfast's centre of gravity was shifting southwards to the White Linen Hall. Chichester Street and Wellington Place – then named North and South Parade – had been started in the 1790s and most of the tall, Georgian, brick houses there were built between 1800 and 1820. On summer evenings the fashionable residents of the area would listen to open-air concerts in front of the White

High Street about 1830: view from the Town Dock, with Hanover Quay (left foreground) and (centre) the last bridge over the Farset.
ULSTER MUSEUM

Linen Hall. Nearby Arthur Street had no shops as yet but it housed the Belfast Theatre which, with the patronage of the 2nd Marquis of Donegall, could afford to invite the leading actors of the day.

Donegall Square South still marked the southern limits of Belfast; beyond it, green fields ran to Sandy Row. The Malone Road was constructed to avoid the steep hills at Stranmillis, and in 1821 the Lisburn Road was completed, providing easier travel south. On the north side of the town the cotton mills' chimneys competed for prominence with the spire of the Poor House. North Queen Street was still the main route to Carrickfergus, and many substantial terraced houses were built here and in York Street in the 1830s. There was no road westwards except a crooked lane, now covered by Clifton Street and Duncairn Street. The Shankill Road, and Ballymacarrett across the Long Bridge, housed the workforce for the mills, glassworks and ropeworks.

High Street remained the main centre of business,

improved by the police boards and the covering of the Farset river to make one broad thoroughfare. A myriad of goods and services were available, there were barber-shops offering 'Easy Shaving and Haircut, Threepence'; chemists with windows full of mysterious coloured bottles; tape sellers crying 'Broad, black or white, twilled or plain, penny tape, at halfpenny a yard!'; McComb's bookshop; street vendors selling tinware, cast-metal goods and earthenware; Mrs McCallum selling tin whistles and marbles to children, tinderboxes, turf and potatoes to their elders; hire firms offering sedan chairs, and taverns such as 'The Mail Coach Passing Through Dromore Square'. At Fountain Street, spring water from Monday's Well in Sandy Row was sold in barrels carried in by donkeys, and Miss McElroy had her emporium of ladies' fashions in Castle Place, beside the town's leading hotels, Wilson's Donegall Arms and Pat Lynn's White Cross.

Belfast's growth was directly linked to the trade passing through its harbour. Customs revenue in 1784 had been £101,876 (including excise) but by 1813 it totalled £393,512 (excluding excise); in 1786, 772 ships totalling 34,287 tons entered the harbour but by 1820 some 2,423 ships entered carrying a total 246,493 tons. If such growth was to continue, the harbour controllers, the Ballast Board, needed to overcome the problem of shallow water between the docks and the Garmoyle Pool which forced many vessels to anchor three miles from the quays. In 1830 the board decided to make two cuts across the bends of the river to make one long straight channel to Garmoyle. Most of the money was raised locally but objections meant that the work did not begin until 1839 and then only on the first part of the project. Nevertheless, Belfast was on the way to becoming one of the world's great ports.

The same appetite for improvement was evident in education. A town meeting in 1806 approved a plan to establish the Academical Institution 'to facilitate and render less expensive the means of acquiring education; to give access to the walks of literature to the middle and lower classes of society; to make provision for the instruction of both sexes'. Lord Donegall made a site available in College Square East, building began in 1810, and Inst, as it became known, opened in 1814 in what is undoubtedly the finest building of the period.

Belfast had numerous private schools catering for the wealthy, but it was not until 1803 that the 'Belfast Weekly or Sunday School' was launched

> ... to afford the means of mental improvement to the children of the lower classes ... teaching them habits of good order and regularity of conduct, in the hope of guarding them from the vices attendant on ignorance and an early course of idleness ...

By 1806, 149 children 'of all religious persuasions' were being taught at the school by fifteen teachers who worked without pay. Four years later, the committee began building a day school in Frederick Street. This was known as the Lancasterian School because it followed Joseph Lancaster's teaching methods: teachers instructed the oldest pupils who in turn taught the next eldest and so on down to the beginners. The project was deemed a success, and a second such school was later established in Brown Square.

Belfast's intellectual and progressive zeal led to the establishment of scientific, scholarly, charitable and self-improvement organisations. In 1821 eight scholars from Inst met in the house of James Drummond,

Professor of Anatomy, to form the Belfast Natural History Society. They quickly accumulated impressive collections of antiquities and botanical, zoological and mineral specimens, and in 1831, aided by public subscriptions, they opened the Belfast Museum of Natural History in College Square North – the first museum in Ireland to be established by public subscription. John Templeton's *Catalogue of Native Plants* and unfinished 'Flora Hibernica' made the museum a treasure-trove for scholars. His son Robert won renown as a zoologist, discovering many new species of insect. The society founded the Botanic Gardens in 1827 (though the handsome palm house – now faithfully restored – was not built until the 1850s).

The Industrial School (1801); the Belfast Literary Society (1801); the House of Industry (1809); the Cosmographical Society (1811); the Anacreontic Society (1814); the General Hospital (1817); the Female Society for the Clothing of the Poor (1820); the Belfast Medical Society (1822); the Mechanics' Institute (1825); the Society for the Relief of the Destitute Sick (1826); and the Belfast Lunatic Asylum (1827) – this is but an incomplete list demonstrating the energy of a growing bourgeoisie with confidence in the future of their town.

Delusions of grandeur led to Belfast being described as 'the Northern Athens'. The poetry of Dr William Drennan (in his poem 'Erin' he coined the phrase 'Emerald Isle') and Samuel Ferguson's novels, inspired by ancient Gaelic legends, were notable successes but the anonymous author of 'Northern Athens, or life in the Emerald Isle, a socio-comico-ludicro-satirical poem' was probably right to ridicule Belfast's pretensions to literary genius. Drennan, Ferguson and the Belfast Society for Promoting Knowledge, which collected books in Irish for its library in the White Linen Hall, demonstrated that the Protestant middle classes' affection for Gaelic Ireland was still alive. Liberal Protestants continued to campaign for the right of Catholics to sit in parliament: in 1818, for example, a town meeting in the Brown Linen Hall called for 'an immediate and total repeal of that part of the penal code which still remains on the statute book against our Catholic fellow-subjects'. However, with the influx of large numbers of Catholics to Belfast and the organisation of the Catholic Association by Daniel O'Connell, such attitudes were set to change.

In 1784 there had been 1,092 Catholics in Belfast, but by 1811 it was observed that of a population of 30,000 'four thousand are Catholics'. As yet there was no sign of sectarian strife. St Patrick's Chapel in Donegall Street, consecrated in 1815, was built with the aid of £530 of Protestant money. Belfast's prosperity contrasted with the economic stagnation of the countryside and drew many seeking employment to the town. By 1835 there were 22,078 Catholics in Belfast, forming more than 33 per cent of the population, compared with 25,939 Presbyterians and 17,942 members of the Church of Ireland. One contemporary wrote: 'within a few years some four or five thousand raw, uneducated Catholic labourers from the south and west had poured into the city'.

O'Connell and the Catholic clergy had become frustrated at the inability of sympathetic Protestants to win emancipation from Westminster. In 1823, therefore, they created the Catholic Association, essentially a populist pressure group, demanding immediate reform. Protestant Ireland was divided: some Protestants continued to support emancipation, believing it would allow Irish Catholics to participate fully in Westminster politics and share the economic benefits of Empire; others were alarmed, fearing that Catholics would use any empowerment to attack Irish Protestants' religion and seize their property. When a local branch of the Catholic Association was set up in Lennon's tavern, Cromac Street, in 1824, Dr Henry Cooke, Moderator of the Presbyterian Synod, testified to a parliamentary inquiry that there was a growing feeling amongst northern Protestants against emancipation: 'with us whenever we hear of the destruction of the Protestant Church, the common people think of the year 1641'.

The alarmed government suppressed the Catholic Association; to avoid a similar fate, the Orange Order reconstituted itself as the Brunswick Clubs. The Belfast Brunswick Club (1828) petitioned parliament to maintain 'the Constitution in its Protestant essentiality'. This was in vain, for in 1829 Westminster voted to allow Catholics to sit in parliament.

Cooke may have failed to stop emancipation, but at the synod of 1827 he drove out Dr Henry Montgomery and the more radical Presbyterians. The *Northern Whig*, formed in 1825 by F. D. Finlay, backed Montgomery and the liberal Protestant stance: the newspaper was instrumental in forming the Reform Society of Belfast in 1830 to support the Whigs who had just come into office at Westminster. These 'wealthy and influential inhabitants' expectantly awaited the reform of parliament and local government and the extension of the franchise; when in October 1831 the Lords rejected the Reform Bill passed by a large majority in the Commons, the *Northern Whig* announced the news with black borders around its pages. The Reform Society denounced the misrepresentation of Belfast:

47

What has our member, Sir Arthur Chichester, ever done for this town? He represents only twelve burgesses. Where have we any record of his talents or his public exertions? No such record exists. He has done nothing for Belfast.

In June 1832 the Reform Bill became law; Belfast's representation at Westminster was increased to two members and for the first time all male owners or tenants of property worth £10 or more could vote. An election was fixed for December 1832. The Whig candidates were William Sharman Crawford and Dr Robert J. Tennent, whilst Lord Arthur Chichester and James Emerson Tennent stood for the Tories. Whigs opposed the privileges of the gentry; Tories lambasted 'ungrateful manufacturers'. The result was a shock for the reformers, with Chichester (848) and J. E. Tennent (737) heading the poll. Both the *Belfast News-Letter* and the *Northern Whig* agreed that only 200 Protestants had voted for R. J. Tennent (613) and Sharman Crawford (597) and that the rest of their votes had come from Catholics.

After the result was announced, a Tory mob attacked the mainly Catholic Hercules Street (now Royal Avenue); the Catholics fought back and four people died after the police opened fire down Hercules Street. Similar incidents became commonplace thereafter: on Christmas Day 1833; after the 1835 election when a Whig linen merchant, John McCance, beat Chichester into third place; and during the July 'marching season' almost every year.

Protestant fears were further aroused in 1834 when O'Connell forced a parliamentary debate calling for the repeal of the Act of Union. Tennent declared that the emancipation movement now stood revealed as 'a mere *ruse de guerre*', a stratagem to establish a Catholic ascendancy and deny Protestants the security of Westminster. In such an atmosphere, Cooke found it easy to lead the Presbyterian majority into a closer alliance with Anglicans. At a meeting in Hillsborough he proclaimed: 'Between the divided churches I publish the banns of a sacred marriage'. The Irish MP C. D. O. Jephson declared, 'we are all divided now into repealers and unionists'. But Westminster rejected repeal, removing any need for Irish Protestants to organise their own political parties, and in Belfast, like in the rest of Ireland, politics remained dominated by Whigs and Tories. Jephson's point was sound enough, however: underneath the surface of the traditional Tory/Whig divide lay the potential for a new form of politics based on sectarian division.

In 1828 Mulholland's York Street cotton mill burned down. When the factory was rebuilt in Henry Street it was not for cotton spinning, however, but for the power spinning of flax. After initial difficulties it had been discovered that a six-hour soaking in cold water made flax slippery enough to be drawn by power-spinning machines into fine yarn without dissolving out the gum. Mulholland and his manager, John Hinds, experimented with flax spinning and after the fire 'it was decided that as English and Scottish competition in the cotton-spinning was so great, and as the linen trade was the natural business of Ireland, it would be advisable in rebuilding the mill to adopt it for the spinning of flax by machinery'. Machinery was made in McAdam's Soho Foundry in Townsend Street and in 1830 the first linen yarn was spun. By 1846 Belfast had twenty-four such mills.

Ireland's linen exports in 1830 had totalled approximately £4.5 million, but in 1857 Belfast's alone reached £9 million and in the boom year of 1865 they rose to £28 million. Cotton had created capital, promoted expertise and attracted a ready workforce from the countryside. Following banking legislation that came into effect in 1824, the Northern, Ulster and Belfast banks had all been able to establish themselves as joint-stock banks; all three had their headquarters in Belfast and were able to provide the linen business with the credit vital for further expansion. The Ulster Railway, running from Great Victoria Street to Lisburn, opened in 1839. The rail network soon expanded to Lurgan and Portadown and, after the Railway Act of 1847, to Ballymena and Holywood (1848), Coleraine and Dublin (1855) and Derry (1860). The conditions for prosperity had been created.

In 1833 the government ordered an inquiry into the municipal corporations of Ireland: Belfast Corporation was highlighted as one of the worst. The burgesses had excluded the freemen from any role in decision making and the constitution had long operated 'virtually to vest the whole of the corporate powers in the lord of the castle of Belfast'. Furthermore, 'No Roman Catholics have been admitted since the relaxation, in the year 1793, of the penal laws previously affecting them.' In short, 'The corporation ... embraces no principle of representation, and confers on the inhabitants no benefit.'

The Irish Municipal Corporations Bill, introduced by Lord Melbourne's Whig government, became law in 1840. Ballymacarrett was combined with Belfast and the new area was divided into five wards, each electing two aldermen and six councillors. One third of the councillors retired each year while half the aldermen stood for re-election triennially. The town clerk had responsibility for the electoral register; men who were rated as £10 householders and who had paid their rates before 31 August were eligible for registration as voters. Belfast at last possessed a representative system of town government.

The first elections took place in 1842. It seemed likely that Catholics would support the Liberals (formerly the Whigs) and that Anglicans would vote for the Conservatives (formerly the Tories); the crucial issue, therefore, was the Presbyterian vote. Following parliament's rejection of repeal of the Union in 1834, O'Connell had worked with successive governments to win reforms, fulfilling the integrationist vision of liberal Protestants. In the 1840s, however, O'Connell's resurrection of the issue of repeal and his creation of a new populist organisation in Ireland, the Repeal Association, to put pressure on Westminster, again raised Protestant fears of Catholic ascendancy. In January 1841, when O'Connell visited Belfast, Dr Henry Cooke challenged him to a public debate on Repeal: 'I believe you are a great bad man engaged in a great bad cause.' Undeterred, O'Connell spoke at Donegall Square, though hecklers interrupted his speech. Later, when he attended a soirée for the St Patrick's Orphan Society in Upper Arthur Street, a Protestant mob attacked St Patrick's chapel in Donegall Street, stoning the homes of known repealers, and besieging the office of O'Connell's newspaper the *Vindicator*, yelling 'To Hell with the Pope!', 'To Hell with the Big Beggarman and his tail!' As police escorted O'Connell from the town, Cooke addressed a massive rally:

> ... within only a comparatively recent period, our town was merely a village. But what a glorious sight does it now present! ... And to what cause is all this prosperity owing? Is it not to the free intercourse which the Union enables us to enjoy with England and Scotland – to that extension of our general commerce which we derive through that channel? ... Can there be any religious liberty, I would ask him, in a community ... where freedom of conscience is unknown?

Fear of Catholic ascendancy and attachment to the economic opportunities of empire had become the foundations of Protestant politics. Consequently, all forty Corporation seats were won by Conservatives.

A Conservative victory had always been likely, but the party's overwhelming dominance was largely attributable to the electoral manipulation of the party's agent, John Bates. Since the parliamentary reforms of 1832, Bates had overseen Conservative registration work, ensuring that supporters were on the electoral register and objecting to the votes of Liberals. In 1835

'Who cares about the bloody blackguards of Sandy Row!' a Repealer cries, but in 1841 Daniel O'Connell needed police protection from the 'bludgeon-men' as they left Donegall Square to catch the mail packet from Donaghadee.
ULSTER MUSEUM

Statue of Henry Cooke outside the Royal Belfast Academical Institution, College Square East: Cooke was a controversial Presbyterian evangelical and a staunch opponent of Catholic emancipation.
PHOTOGRAPH: BRIAN HUGHES

he had eighty Liberals disenfranchised because they described their premises as 'house and shop' instead of 'house, shop'. His organisation of ward associations compared favourably with the disorganisation and incompetence of Belfast Liberals. At the new Corporation's first meeting Bates was elected town clerk, a post that gave him official control over registration.

Between 1831 and 1841 Belfast's population had grown by 32.2 per cent to over 70,000: a decade later the total was 87,000. The Corporation had responsibility for providing improvements and services for this burgeoning population. Their zeal for improvement made Belfast councillors the most progressive Conservatives in Ireland, perhaps even in the United Kingdom. By 1848 only 29 of 178 municipal corporations in England and Wales had applied for additional powers to initiate improvements; even the Manchester radicals objected to the costs of 'cursed improvements'. By contrast Belfast Corporation secured legislation to take over the powers of the Police Committee and Commissioners (1844) and to borrow up to £150,000 (1845). Money was spent widening streets, building new streets, paving, cleaning and lighting the town, laying sewers, buying land for markets and providing fire engines.

In this respect Protestant radicalism remained alive, but such reforming zeal was only possible because Protestants felt secure in their control of the Corporation and because infrastructural improvements did not provide political empowerment for Catholics. The Corporation extended its powers: it obtained the right to set up a gasworks and borrow another £50,000 (1846); 'An Act for the Further Improvement of the Borough' (1847); and further borrowing powers to pay for the 'the abatement of the [river] Blackstaff nuisance' (1850). Minimum housing standards were laid down and support was given to the Factory Acts of 1847 and 1850 which restricted the working day to ten hours. New markets sprang up, particularly at May's Fields, and Corporation and Victoria streets were built.

The relief of poverty was not part of the Corporation's remit. In 1836 a government inquiry had painted a grim picture of poverty in Ireland, where no official system of poor relief existed. Belfast's private charities, the Clifton Street Poor House and the House of Industry, received praise but their provision of accommodation, food and tools merely scratched the surface. In 1838, therefore, the government established Poor Law 'unions' throughout Ireland, based on the English system of indoor relief; those seeking assistance would have to go to live in a workhouse. These workhouses, thought by many to be inappropriate for rural Ireland, were to be governed by Boards of Guardians elected by the ratepayers.

The Belfast Union extended to the surrounding districts. A site was bought on the Lisburn Road for £2,130 and a well-equipped workhouse, accommodating 1,000 inmates, was built for £10,122. Contemporary morality and political philosophy demanded a harsh environment. All inmates had to do work that encouraged 'a dislike to remain in the workhouse', food was deliberately inferior to that available to local labourers, discipline was by contemporary standards severe, and families were broken up by the segregation of the sexes. This harsh regime and good employment opportunities kept Belfast's workhouse population at manageable levels, but the economy throughout the rest of Ireland was less sound.

In 1845 blight struck the potato crop over much of Ireland. The next year the crop failed almost completely and by the winter of 1846-47 millions faced destitution. Belfast's prosperity made it a magnet for the destitute. The *Belfast News-Letter* reported that 'starving wretches hourly swarm into the streets from the country'. With them came fever. Typhus was the most deadly, reaching epidemic proportions by 1847. Leading citizens established a Board of Health but their efforts were never enough. Dr Malcolm noted that 'one out of every five persons in Belfast was attacked [by fever] during this year'. The Shankill and Friar's Bush burying grounds were full. The total numbers who died in Belfast of famine and fever cannot be known. The government allowed the Belfast Union to provide 'outdoor relief' in the form of soup kitchens, but Lord John Russell, the prime minister, declared, 'It must be thoroughly understood that we cannot feed the people.'

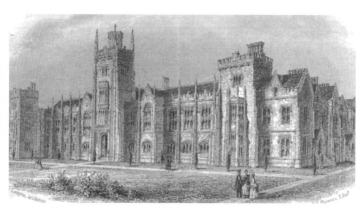

An 1850s engraving of Queen's College, Belfast: the college was designed by
Charles Lanyon and established in 1845.
BRIAN WALKER

Belfast was a Janus town, both Irish and British.
Industrialisation and the social conditions that resulted
from industrialisation made it comparable to Glasgow,
Liverpool and other British cities. Many visitors observed that the town was not typical of Ireland. Mr and
Mrs S. C. Hall wrote thus in 1843: 'The cleanly and
bustling appearance of Belfast is decidedly un-national.
That it is in Ireland but not of it is a remark ever on the
lips of visitors from south or west.' H. D. Inglis concluded that 'the town and its neighbouring districts
have nothing in common with the rest of Ireland'. Yet
the experience of famine and continued religious and
political rivalries, intensified by the influx of people
from the countryside who brought their generations-
old feuds with them, marked Belfast as an Irish town.
When Queen Victoria visited Belfast in 1849, thousands
greeted 'Erin's own Queen'. It was a dual identity
which was to dominate the town's future.

One stop on the royal party's tour was the new
Queen's College. This had been established in 1845 to

provide Ulster with a higher education establishment. Supposedly non-denominational, the college took on a Presbyterian character just as sister colleges in Galway and Cork became predominantly Catholic. Charles Lanyon, described as 'the greatest single name in the development of Belfast', drew inspiration from the Oxford colleges in designing Queen's. Indeed, Lanyon's achievements, such as the Queen's Bridge (1843), the Deaf and Dumb Institution (1845), the old Exchange refurbished for the Ulster Bank (1845), Crumlin Road Gaol (1846), the County Courthouse (1850), the Northern Bank headquarters in Queen's Square (1852), the Assembly's College (1853), the Custom House (1857) and the Ulster Club in Castle Place (1862), represented, in bricks and mortar, the confidence and ebullience of Belfast's middle classes. His main rival, W. J. Barre from Newry, initiated a Gothic revival, building the Unitarian Church in York Street (1855), the Ulster Hall (1860), the Provincial Bank of Ireland in Castle Place, the Albert Memorial (known to all as the Albert Clock) and Belfast Castle on the slopes of Cave Hill (all 1867). Both men also built new churches, and mansions for the middle classes in the

PUBLISHED BY W. H. LIZARS, EDIN.

Vignette showing (from left) St Anne's Parish Church, the new Queen's Bridge (1843), and Fisherwick Presbyterian Church.

The Queen's Bridge, Belfast, in 1860: the Lagan has been widened and deepened to make the Victoria Channel, enabling the ships seen here to come up to the quays. On the right is the Belfast & County Down railway terminus and on the left is Charles Lanyon's Custom House.
ULSTER MUSEUM

Malone suburb.

The harbour was an icon of Belfast's improvement. In 1841 the first cut from Dunbar's Dock (at the northern end of Corporation Street) had been completed and the excavated mud was heaped on the eastern side of the river to make Queen's Island: this became the town's main pleasure park with an amusement committee that organised an annual fête. And in 1849 the engineer William Dargan oversaw the second cut, named the Victoria Channel, which gave easy access to the docks from Garmoyle Pool. Even this was inadequate, however, as trade continued to increase: tonnage rose from 288,143 in 1837 to 538,525 in 1847, whilst the value of exports and imports rose from £5.7 million in 1836 to £12.6 million in 1852. Land was reclaimed and new docks were opened, and by 1867 Belfast was handling 1.3 million tons of shipping.

The Conservative councillors' policy of getting 'the largest amount of good done at the least possible expense' had kept rates low, but Liberals disliked the fact that the Corporation defrayed debts by buying private property, improving it and selling it for profit. Liberals thus helped to block the Blackstaff drainage scheme in 1850. A government inquiry in 1852 reported that the Corporation's powers had been 'judiciously exercised for the improvement of the borough' and recommended that the borough be extended from 1.5 square miles to 10 square miles to account for population growth. The suburbs were now rated and regulated and further improvements were made possible.

The Liberals were hopelessly divided: Catholics wanted urban improvements, whilst Protestant employers resented the rate increase brought about by the boundary extension. They were united only in opposition to town clerk Bates. In 1853 they accused the Conservatives of misappropriating funds, fraud and embezzlement, forcing Bates's resignation in 1855: three months later he died. At the 1855 election six Liberals were returned, including the first Catholic, Bernard Hughes. A Royal Commission of 1859 rejected most of the charges against the Conservatives but the party was in disarray without Bates and seventeen Liberals were returned that year. In 1861 Liberals won half the seats and Sir Edward Coey became Belfast's first and last Liberal mayor. The Liberals did not build a party machine, however, and Conservatives subsequently reorganised and attended to the register, reducing the Liberals to five seats in 1864.

The prosperity enjoyed by the middle classes was not shared by the labouring masses. A report by the Sanitary Committee in 1849 found the Dock area in a 'filthy, flooded, and neglected state', while Sandy Row, the Pound, Cromac, Ballymacarrett, Smithfield and New

Lodge all had 'large cesspools and open drains'. Dr Malcolm's report of 1852 concluded that bad drainage was the major sanitation problem; he estimated that only 3,000 of the 10,000 homes in the town had piped water. The Reverend W. M. O'Hanlon's *Walks Among the Poor of Belfast* (1853) confirmed this picture. Together they made a case for improved sanitation; Malcolm showed that, in 1847, 70 per cent of houses 'deficient in sewerage' had fever but only 19 per cent of houses in the better-drained districts suffered. Belfast indeed had much in common with cities like Liverpool, Bristol, Edinburgh and Glasgow: bye-laws, age structure, cholera epidemics in 1831–32 and 1848–49, prostitution and alcoholism, medical and Poor Law systems, including vaccination, and private philanthropy. Mortality rates in Belfast were much higher, however: O'Hanlon calculated that 'absolutely excessive' infant mortality meant that the average life expectancy was nine years.

Exposed machinery, unhealthy conditions and employers' persistent breaches of regulations made the linen mills, which employed mainly women and children, a dangerous environment. Exhausted workers, who started at 5 a.m. and finished at 7 or 8 p.m., could lose a hand in the hackling machine; the flax dust, or 'pouce', affected the lungs so much that the army would not enlist young men who had worked in the mills. Workers in the hot, steamy spinning room were prone to lung disease, 'mill fever', swollen legs, and 'papular' and 'pastular' eruptions. Even the better-paid weavers suffered from chest infections.

Elections and other political events provided occasion for mobs of Protestant and Catholic labourers to confront each other on a regular basis. At a Twelfth of July service in Christ Church in 1857, the Reverend Dr

Mid-nineteenth-century sectarian rioting in Sandy Row (artist unknown):
the Boyne Bridge formed the frontier with the Catholic Pound.
ULSTER MUSEUM

Drew denounced 'the arrogant pretences of Popes and
the outrageous dogmata of their blood-stained
religion'. The church stood between Sandy Row and
the Pound and a Catholic mob attacked the police on
patrol outside, sparking off ten days of continuous rioting. Shootings followed and a Catholic mill girl was
killed. Similar violence erupted in August 1864 when
Protestants attacked a train carrying Catholics returning
from a Dublin ceremony to commemorate O'Connell.
Continuous conflict around Sandy Row and the Pound
forced the closure of local mills and factories that
month. On 15 August, around 400 Catholics looted
Belfast gunsmiths and attacked Brown Square
National School. Protestant workers in nearby factories
surged out and repelled the invaders and took revenge
on St Malachy's Chapel. The mobs were only dispersed
by cavalry charges.

The *Northern Whig* blamed Catholic navvies and

called for radical action: 'The prosperity of our town . . . brought to it for the formation of our new docks this horde of assassins; and the greatest punishment that could be inflicted upon them would be . . . to dismiss them, and send them starving from our town, as starving they came to it.' During the days that followed, Protestant shipwrights from the Shankill joined the fray, plundering gunsmiths and attacking St Peter's pro-cathedral in the Falls and Catholic navvies in the shipyards. The conflict ended with many wounded and at least twelve killed.

Inquiries castigated Orange festivals and the partiality of the Protestant-dominated Town Police, which was replaced by the Royal Irish Constabulary, but this did not explain the violence. Migration from rural Ulster, which boosted Catholic numbers in Belfast to about 30 per cent of the population from the 1830s, and O'Connell's organised challenge to the Union, caused many Belfast Protestants to reassess the idealism of their parents. Politicians such as Bates did not create sectarian bitterness, which went back generations, they simply provided organisation. Similarly, political events merely provided a scheduled meeting place for rival mobs to confront each other.

Around 1800 the Orange Order had been weak in Belfast but by 1851 there were 35 lodges with 1,335 members; in 1864 Belfast became a County Grand Lodge. This reflected a more general growth in religious fervour amongst Protestants: street preachers attracted huge audiences and 35,000 people attended a meeting in Botanic Gardens during the Great Revival of 1859. Catholics also joined fraternal societies, such as the Fenian Brotherhood, preaching separation from Britain. Social deprivation and unemployment were incidental in such circumstances: the depression of 1857 came *after* the riots of that year, while in 1864 Belfast was in the middle of a linen boom.

During the American Civil War the cotton-growing states of America were devastated and the Lancashire mills were starved of raw material. Linen was the best substitute, and Belfast's production soared. Post-Famine emigration had reduced the surplus of labour available to employers and forced up wages. Consequently, power looms became more attractive, the 4,900 looms operative in 1861 surpassing the total for Britain. The normalisation of cotton production in 1867 increased competition and Belfast was forced temporarily to cut its linen production; 4,000 of the 12,000 looms soon stood idle. Expecting the boom to continue, the industry had borrowed heavily and overextended its capacity. Nevertheless, Belfast was now the greatest centre of linen production in the world. It was a success story that engineering and shipbuilding were set to build upon.

5
IMPERIAL CITY
1870–1921

In the first part of the nineteenth century, Cork had been Ireland's shipbuilding centre, but the 1850s improvements to Belfast's port provided deep water and a perfect site, Queen's Island, for a shipbuilding yard. In 1853 the Harbour Commissioners built a yard on the island for Robert Hickson, an ironmaster who saw shipbuilding as an ideal outlet for his iron plate. Hickson therefore needed an expert manager, and soon found Edward Harland, a 23-year-old Yorkshireman who had learned his trade at shipyards on the Tyne and Clyde, to fill the role. The yard flourished, and after Harland had failed to establish his own yard in Liverpool, he succeeded in buying out Hickson for £5,000. This money was supplied by G. C. Schwabe, who joined the firm along with his nephew Gustav Wolff. It was Harland, however, who supplied the managerial and engineering expertise that were the basis of the yard's future success.

Throughout the 1860s Harland & Wolff built a series of ocean-going ships which, thanks to Harland's design, possessed greater capacity and speed than rival ships. In 1870 a contract was signed with the Oceanic Steam Navigation Company of Liverpool, better known as the White Star Line, to supply transatlantic liners powered by compound engines and screw propulsion. Providing luxury for first-class passengers, cheap fares for emigrants, and record-breaking speed, the *Oceanic* (1870) and later the *Germanic* and the *Britannic* (1874), made all other North Atlantic liners obsolete. The workforce rose from 500 in 1861 to 2,400 in 1870, and in 1880 the company extended the yard to 40 acres and built its own engine works.

Edward Harland and Gustav Wolff gradually handed control of the firm to others as they became immersed in public life: both were Conservative MPs for Belfast, and in 1885–86 Harland was mayor. William Pirrie and Walter Wilson provided the managerial skill and technical expertise necessary to compete in the new age of steel ships. The company suffered during a trade depression in 1881–85, laying off 1,500 workers and forcing others to accept wage cuts, but by 1889, with the launch of the *Majestic* and the *Teutonic*, it was once again setting the example for others to follow. In the 1890s output rose to an average 100,000 tons a year and the workforce grew to 9,000, a success story that overshadowed the growth of other Belfast yards such as Workman Clark & Company, affectionately known as 'the wee yard'. Continued improvements by the Harbour Commissioners, such as the opening of new docks and the depressing and widening of the channel, enabled further expansion.

Linen, however, remained Belfast's largest employer. Some 55,000 people were employed in the Irish linen industry in 1871, 62,000 in 1885, and 69,000 in 1896: Belfast had over 80 per cent of Ireland's spindles and 70 per cent of power looms, and only a small proportion of the country's millworkers worked outside the city. Throughout the last quarter of the nineteenth century, linen prices declined steadily as foreign tariffs damaged exports and cheaper cotton captured markets. Linen production required four times as many operatives as cotton, and governments were introducing regulatory legislation. Millowners therefore believed that wages had to be kept down. The average wage was 11s. 0d. in

1875, 10s. 6d. in 1884, 11s. 0d. in 1886 and 12s. 0d. in 1906. Skilled men earned more, but 68 per cent of linen workers were women and 26 per cent were juveniles.

The mechanisation and modernisation of linen and shipbuilding were instrumental in helping Belfast develop an engineering industry. Belfast's iron foundries had developed in the first half of the nineteenth century until by 1870 there were twenty. British foundries sold cheaper domestic goods, forcing Belfast to concentrate on machine production: by 1910 only two of the city's eighteen foundries were not engaged in engineering. Steam engines, water turbines, electricity generators, steam pumps, piston rings, electric dynamos and engines for cotton mills were made in Belfast and sold in Britain and abroad. Belfast could not compete with Manchester and Leeds in the making of cotton machinery and linen looms, but it did become the

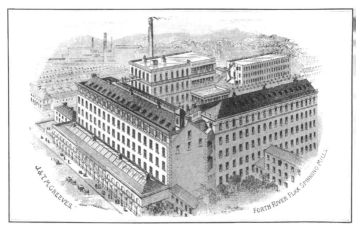

J. and T.M. Greeves, Forth River Flax Spinning Mills: by 1896 the Irish linen industry was employing 69,000 people.

Workers from Charter's spinning mill, North Howard Steet, *c.* 1915. The men are fitters who looked after the machines.

world leader for the production of linen machinery. James Mackie & Sons, and Combe Barbour were the two largest engineering companies outside the shipyards and between them they made the full range of flax machinery; local spinners visited the foundries 'to point out their exact requirements and the defects of previous machines'.

Other companies thrived in this period. Musgrave Brothers provided luxury stable and house fittings for, amongst others, the Prince of Wales; the Sirocco Works was the world leader in ventilation and fan manufacture, and Thomas Gallaher produced tobacco spinning machinery and cigarettes. By the end of the nineteenth century the Belfast Ropeworks, established in 1872, was the biggest in the world. Mass production methods were introduced to whiskey distilling at the Royal Irish Distilleries plant of Dunville and Craig, and at the Irish Distillery at Connswater and the

Avoniel Distillery, so that by 1900 Belfast accounted for 60 per cent of Irish whiskey exports. Companies such as the Union Foundry and Joseph Braddell & Son produced spades, nails and guns. Mill owners such as the Ewarts, Mulhollands, Charters and Malcolmsons laid out streets of cheap houses near their factories in the Falls, Sandy Row and Shankill. In the 1870s, working-class housing extended from Agnes Street, Northumberland Street and Albert Street to Bridge End, Connswater and Ormeau. Often poorly built and insanitary, these houses were condemned in 1873 by one medical officer as 'not fit to afford shelter to domesticated animals'. The major problem was that linen workers were so poorly paid that families had to sublet rooms to fellow workers; even then, they could afford only a subsistence diet of 'tea and white bread three times daily ... potatoes or meat rarely'. Corporation regulations to improve sewage, paving and building specifications were helpful but slow to develop. The higher wages commanded by the growing numbers of skilled artisans in the new heavy industries became crucial in ensuring that a greater proportion of workers could afford to rent better accommodation.

In the 1880s the clusters of working-class housing expanded around the mills, foundries and engineering works, particularly in the west and north. In the 1890s the gaps between these clusters were filled to form a 'continuously built-up area of low-rental housing' which

> stretched from the Bog Meadows at Donegall Road in the west to the Woodstock and Beersbridge Road area in the east, and from the Skegoniel district on York Road in the north to the Essex Street area off the Ormeau Road in the south.

So-called parlour houses, with tiny front gardens, decorative tiles and one room more than kitchen houses, were built between the Ballygomartin and Woodvale roads, and in Manor Street and Cliftonpark Avenue in the north; around Alexandra Park and Gainsborough Drive in the north-west; near the Ravenhill Road and Cregagh Road in the east; and at Stranmillis in the south.

In the 1850s and 1860s, fashionable villas had been erected for the wealthy few who had carriages or who could pay for the horse-drawn omnibus, on radial routes such as the Lisburn, Antrim, Ormeau and Crumlin roads. The Belfast Street Tramways Company, founded in 1872, laid tracks for horse-drawn trams and by the 1880s it was supplying a service running at five-minute intervals on main routes and costing 2d. for one journey; in 1892 the price fell to 1d. A network of tracks ran to the suburbs, which were increasingly occupied by the business and professional classes who could now commute to their businesses in the inner-city area. South Belfast, along the Lisburn and Malone roads, became the most fashionable residential area; the Antrim Road expanded in the north, while in the east developers built new houses in Mountpottinger, Ormeau, Ballynafeigh and Rosetta.

A striking feature of the building boom in Belfast was that dwellings were built ahead of demand, and many remained unsold for years. Most of the developers were professional speculators and builders, but some of Belfast's leading landowners and leaseholders, such as the Marquis of Downshire, Baron Templemore and the Ashmores, also contributed. The linen lords did not: as soon as the Corporation had regulated building standards and made landlords responsible for repairs, they ceased to build for their workers. Building societies and investment companies provided alternatives. R. J. McConnell & Company was selling kitchen houses in the Shankill in lots of five for £345 while selling villas in Rosetta Park for £700 each. H. & J. Martin was the biggest builder, contractor and brick maker in Belfast, controlling 300 acres of building land across the city in areas such as Malone, Ormeau, Ravenhill, Rosetta, Donegall Road, Cregagh and the Shankill. Supplied with cheap labour and low-cost, imported raw materials, Belfast grew rapidly.

In 1888 Belfast was granted a royal charter and became a city, recognition that it was not only the largest town in Ireland and the first in manufacturing and commerce but also the third port in the United Kingdom, its customs revenue exceeded by only Liverpool and London. The Corporation responded with a series of civic improvements: rebuilding the Queen's Bridge which had collapsed; opening the Ormeau, Falls, Dunville, Victoria, Woodvale and Alexandra parks to the public; and in 1894 purchasing the site for an asylum at Purdysburn. The splendid free public library built in Royal Avenue, now fast developing as a prime

Ormeau Park, south Belfast, in the early twentieth century
DAVID BURNETT

Life is difficult for the horse-drawn trams in a flooded Donegall
Square, c. 1895
PUBLIC RECORD OFFICE OF NORTHERN IRELAND

commercial site, provided a public counterpart to
grandiose private constructions such as the Robinson &
Cleaver department store at Donegall Place. Between
1887 and 1894 new sewers were laid for the whole city,
and in 1893 the Belfast Water Commissioners began
their great project to pipe Mourne water to Belfast. Until the scheme was completed in 1901, however, water
pollution persisted; in 1897 it contributed to an outbreak of typhoid that affected 27,000 people.

Belfast's confidence was displayed in science rather
than in the arts. Painters such as J. W. Carey were com-
petent recorders of the city's growth but never rose to
prominence. In contrast, Sir Almroth Wright became
an internationally renowned pathologist and bacteriol-
ogist, and William Thomson (created Lord Kelvin in
1892) did more than anyone else in Britain to lay the
foundations of modern physics. Inventors such as

Thomas Romney Robinson, who designed the cup anemometer to measure wind speed, and John Boyd Dunlop, who made the first working pneumatic tyre, were held in special affection. Dunlop's Belfast company, established in 1890, became the basis of a multi-national firm.

The economic gains enjoyed by Belfast's skilled male artisans were augmented by political reforms such as the 1867 Reform Act which gave them the vote. 'What if the serfs should get the upper hand over their masters?' asked the *Northern Whig*. Protestant workers dominated the new industries and they were angry with Belfast's Conservative MPs whom they deemed to be doing little to safeguard or further their interests. Consequently they helped elect an Orange populist, William Johnston, and a Liberal, Thomas McClure. The Conservative bosses later co-operated with Johnston and thus secured the election of the shipowner J. P. Corry, but it was Johnston's populist Protestantism, exemplified in his support for the 1874 Factory Act and for repeal of the Party Processions Act prohibiting Orange marches, that represented most accurately the political views of Protestant workers.

On 15 August 1872, Catholics gathered in the Pound, the Falls and in Hercules Street to participate in Belfast's first nationalist parade. The parade was led by Joseph Gillis Biggar, a member of the Corporation, chairman of the Board of Water Commissioners and president of the Belfast Home Rule Association, who pleased the 30,000 crowd at Hannahstown by calling for the release of Fenian prisoners. Nationalism had enjoyed popular support among Catholics in the 1860s, but confidence had been undermined by the militant Fenians' failed rebellion of 1867. The Home Rule ideal supported by

Biggar envisaged a self-governing parliament in Dublin in which Irishmen of every religion could decide their future without Westminster's interference. At grass-roots level, however, complex political formulae were reduced to simplistic sectarian confrontation: Catholics expected to gain and Protestants expected to lose from such arrangements. Belfast's Protestant artisans were increasingly loyal to Britain, the source of their prosperity and political reform as well as security against future rebellion, and they reacted angrily to Biggar's demonstration.

That night Protestants emerged from Sandy Row and clashed with Catholics from the Pound near Great Victoria Street railway terminus. By midnight the casualty wards of Frederick Street General Hospital were full. Over the next six days there were ongoing riots, shootings and attacks on churches and houses. The large-scale eviction of Catholics living in Protestant areas and of Protestants living in Catholic areas reflected the depth of divisions in Belfast.

Electoral reforms in 1884 and 1885 trebled Ireland's electorate and redistributed parliamentary seats: Belfast was divided into four constituencies. At the 1885 election Johnston won South Belfast; E. S. Cobain, an Orange candidate, defeated the Conservative, J. P. Corry, in East Belfast; Sir William Ewart won North Belfast for the Conservatives; and in West Belfast the Conservative, J. H. Haslett, defeated the Nationalist, Thomas Sexton, by only 37 votes. But under Charles Stewart Parnell the Home Rule movement had so developed that the Irish Parliamentary Party – the Nationalists – was now Ireland's major political party: it returned 85 MPs, and held the balance of power in parliament between Conservatives and Liberals.

W. E. Gladstone, the Liberal leader, announced his conversion to Home Rule in January 1886, causing Liberals who favoured maintaining the Union to leave the party *en masse* and form an alliance with Conservatives. Irish Unionists became an important part of this UK-wide alliance after Belfast Liberals such as Adam Duffin and Thomas Sinclair led the vast majority of Irish Liberals into alliance with Irish Conservatives. Duffin and Sinclair saw themselves as the political inheritors of Belfast's eighteenth-century radicalism: their forefathers had rejected Anglican ascendancy then, and they would reject Catholic ascendancy now.

On 22 February 1886, the prominent Conservative Lord Randolph Churchill spoke at a monster demonstration of Unionists in Belfast's Ulster Hall. Shortly afterwards he coined the phrase 'Ulster will fight and Ulster will be right', but popular organisation against Home Rule was made unnecessary by the defeat of Gladstone's bill in the House of Commons on 8 June, thanks to the votes of Liberal Unionists. The writer Frankfort Moore received the news in Belfast by electric telegraph and on his way home met Protestant workers who had risen early and come

> ... from their homes to learn the result of the division in the House of Commons; and when I told them that the Bill had been defeated, the cheers that filled the air at the news surprised the policemen at the corners. ... I met scores of the same class of the population who ... put to me in their own idiom and staccato pronunciation the burning question:
>
> 'Is them 'uns bate?'
>
> And when I assured them that the unspeakable Nationalists had been beaten by a good majority, once more cheers were raised.

The intensity of feeling expressed was real. On 4 June, shipwrights had converged on Alexandra dock and exacted lethal revenge on Catholic navvies who had expelled a Protestant with the warning that Home Rule would mean that 'none of the Orange sort would get leave to work or earn a loaf of bread in Belfast'. The RIC, composed mainly of southern Catholics though officered mainly by Protestants, struggled to keep rival mobs apart over the next few days and came under assault from Protestants who viewed them as partisan. On 9 June, the Bower's Hill RIC barracks on the Shankill was attacked so fiercely that officers began firing indiscriminately at the mob: seven people were killed but only two had been rioting. Protestant demands grew for the restoration of local policing. Violence resumed on 13–14 July when mobs from the Shankill and Falls clashed; the confrontations resulted in four more deaths. Both Protestant and Catholic church outings were attacked by hostile gangs at the end of the month, sparking a week of violence in which thirteen people died. The following weekend almost all the Catholic workers in the shipyards were driven out, and another twelve people were killed in riots. Violence continued until heavy rains in mid-September 'took the heart out of the fighting'. About fifty people had been killed in that summer's disturbances, the most deadly episode in Ireland in the nineteenth century.

In 1892, a second political crisis seemed imminent when Salisbury's Conservative government resigned. A general election was called and Gladstone, again promoting Home Rule, was favourite to win. Irish Unionists were anxious that their cause should not be discredited in Britain by violence as it had been in 1886. An Ulster Convention League was formed,

The Ulster Unionist Convention, Botanic Gardens, 17 June 1892
ULSTER SOCIETY

inspired by Belfast's Liberal Unionist leaders, and Unionists were organised into a peaceful show of strength at the Ulster Unionist Convention in Botanic Gardens on 17 June 1892. Approximately 12,000 delegates from across Ulster attended, supported by tens of thousands of spectators. A special hall, covering an acre of ground, had been erected and decorated; in order to ensure an atmosphere of solemnity and order, there were no boisterous Orange bands and songs. Speakers stressed political and economic objections to Home Rule rather than the religious question. But the Ulster Unionist Convention prevented neither Gladstone's election victory nor the passage of Home Rule through the Commons in 1893. Unionist power remained with the gentry in the Lords, where the bill was quickly defeated. When Conservatives and Liberal Unionists won the 1895 election and formed a Unionist government, the enthusiasm for a more popular and representative Unionist Party in Ulster evaporated. It was clear, none the less, that if such a body was deemed necessary some time in the future, Belfast would be its focal point.

Despite its industrial character, Belfast did not have an organised labour movement until relatively late. The Belfast Trades Council formed in 1881 was dominated by small craft unions and concerned with negotiating pay and conditions rather than socialist politics. Shipyard engineers were not represented until 1889, and the trades council made no effort to organise unskilled workers. British-based unions, such as the Gasworkers' Union and the National Amalgamated Union of Labour, organised the unskilled in the 1890s, but efforts to create unions for female linen workers failed. The idea that employers made unions weak by fostering sectarian divisions is incorrect. When linen-lappers went on strike in 1892, the mill owners locked them out and replaced them with machines and women. This was in spite of the alliance of 'Orangeman ... arm in arm beside his Nationalist fellow workman' which the *Northern Whig* characterised as 'a power that must be reckoned with'. And the 10,000 predominantly Protestant shipyard engineers on strike in 1895–96 won few concessions from employers.

Sectarian divisions were maintained by the workers themselves who insisted on keeping certain trades exclusively Protestant or exclusively Catholic. Skilled trades such as shipbuilding and engineering employed about 25 per cent of Belfast's workforce and were overwhelmingly Protestant because, as in Britain, they exercised their long-established right to select apprentices: neither employers nor government interfered with this procedure, which inevitably favoured family and friends. Amongst the remaining masses, there were at least as many unskilled and low-paid Protestants as

Catholics. The former organised occupational Orange lodges, such as the Belfast Paviors Purple Star and the Belfast Stone Cutters, to give themselves an employment advantage. Although they had fewer institutions, Catholics maintained disproportionate advantage amongst general labourers, flax spinners and dockers. Co-operation amongst Protestants and Catholics, as in 1892, the year of the Ulster Unionist Convention, was for mutual economic benefit, and not the beginning of a new form of politics.

In 1902 William Johnston died and Tom Sloan, leader of the Belfast Protestant Association (BPA), decided to contest the vacant South Belfast seat. The BPA was a working-class Protestant organisation which accused Irish Unionist leaders of being a wealthy elite more concerned with their own interests and party politics in London than with representing the Protestant masses. Sloan won the seat against the Unionist Party candidate. Similar criticisms against the Orange Order led to his suspension: subsequently Sloan formed the Independent Orange Order, unconnected to any political party; 20 of its 55 lodges were in Belfast.

A Belfast branch of the Labour Representation Committee, formed in 1903, targeted North Belfast for an electoral assault. William Walker, a trade unionist and socialist, was selected as candidate. During the recession of 1904–5, which saw unemployment rise in the shipyards, the incumbent Unionist MP, Sir James Haslett, died: the Unionist candidate chosen to succeed him, the Lord Mayor Sir Daniel Dixon, was a timber merchant and shipowner widely regarded as hostile to labour who seemed to offer Walker the perfect target for a by-election. Dixon's line was to question Walker's association with the British Labour Party, which

Jim Larkin addressing supporters in Queen's Square during the 1907 dock strike.

supported Home Rule. This prompted Sloan's BPA to demand clarification from Walker, who was forced to declare for the Union. Unconvinced, the Imperial Protestant Federation presented Walker with a questionnaire on religion; his replies were published in the *Northern Whig*. Over 1,000 nationalist votes were estimated to have been lost by Walker's Protestant and Unionist sympathies and Dixon won the seat, a result repeated in the general election of 1906. The class-based politics increasingly evident in Britain also existed in Belfast, only here it was confined within the limitations imposed by unionism and nationalism.

The most determined effort to break this pattern came in 1907 when James Larkin of the National Union of Dock Labourers arrived from Liverpool to organise unskilled workers such as the carters and dockers. A strike by dockers in May was indicative of increasing militancy; employers responded with a lockout and the importation of blackleg labour from Britain. Other workers went on strike in sympathy and by the summer Larkin was addressing huge crowds, enthusing that he, a Catholic and a nationalist, was leading men who were Protestant and Unionist. But as far as Belfast's workers were concerned, trade unions were for settling economic rather than political issues: they returned to work after the carters had secured a wage increase and the bruised dockers' union had negotiated its recognition by employers. In so doing the Belfast workers returned to their traditional political positions and rejected the idea of a cross-sectarian socialist party. The major political developments were taking place within unionism and nationalism, as working-class pressure induced leaders to establish more representative structures, such as the Ulster Unionist Council (UUC) and the Ancient Order of Hibernians, and to adopt more trenchantly sectarian positions.

One of the main reasons for working-class discontent in Edwardian Belfast was the increased cost of living. From 1870 to the end of the century food prices had fallen so that even poorly paid flax workers experienced a rise of about 200 per cent in their purchasing power; between 1895 and 1912, however, food prices increased by 29 per cent, forcing the unskilled to spend almost 60 per cent of their wages on food. The construction of new housing for the working class also declined; the 1,303 houses built in 1907 amounted to only 28 per cent of the number built in 1898. By 1907 those builders who were not bankrupt were concentrating on dwellings for the better-off in the suburbs. The demise of private housing for the working classes led the Corporation to subsidise slum clearance and new public housing in Brown Square, Institution Place, and John and Hamill streets.

Middle-class housing was erected by the Bloomfield Company and H. & J. Martin at Knock, Malone, Ballygomartin and Bloomfield, and between the Antrim Road and the Shore and Somerton roads. The

Corporation's Tramways and Electricity Committee bought out the Belfast Street Tramways Company in 1904 for £307,500 and electrified the tram network. In 1906 there was forty miles of track, and the penny-fare cars carried not only the shipyard workers to Queen's Island but also middle-class commuters to and from suburbs such as Cliftonville Garden Village, where houses cost around £350. Although the demand for suburban homes eventually slackened, by the end of the First World War Belfast stretched for six miles from north to south and seven miles from east to west.

Belfast's population had risen from 174,412 in 1871 to 349,180 in 1901 and 386,947 in 1911. Touring companies of entertainers could not ignore the British Empire's fastest-growing city, and the popular theatre of variety shows and melodrama delighted audiences. The Grand Opera House opened in 1895, a splendid theatre reflecting Belfast's status as Ireland's largest and richest city; it was able to attract celebrated performers such as Sarah Bernhardt, Beerbohm Tree and Forbes-Robertson. Protestant intellectuals such as Bulmer Hobson were inspired by the Gaelic cultural revival and in 1904 formed the Ulster Literary Society. Although it never found a permanent home, the society did much to encourage indigenous creative talent such as Rutherford Mayne and Gerald MacNamara. Forest Reid's novels, portraying the rites of passage of suburban youth, made him the city's first novelist to win widespread recognition.

Reid's work largely ignored the political and socio-economic realities of Belfast, described by the *Daily Mail* in 1903 as 'a commercial cockpit where sordid little struggles are continuously in progress'. The departure of the middle classes to the suburbs left commerce dominating the city centre. Four of the city's large department stores were built by local businessmen; two of them, Anderson & McAuley and Robinson & Cleaver, had branches in Britain. There were also chain stores, such as Tylers (shoes) and Home and Colonial Stores, and British companies, such as Thorntons (waterproofs), Lizars (opticians), Sawers (fish, meat, poultry), James Nelson & Sons and the River Plate Company (frozen meat). Cantrell & Cochrane aerated and bottled Belfast spring water which was drunk throughout the Empire. Architecturally, however, the city developed little. Fisherwick Church became the headquarters of the Presbyterian Church when its congregation moved to a new building on the Malone Road, while St Anne's Church was demolished and a new but uninspiring Anglican cathedral of the same name was built on the site. The Technical College built in front of Inst was later described by Charles Brett as 'the largest and most ornate cuckoo's egg ever laid in a songbird's nest'; the Scottish Provident, Scottish Temperance and Northern Bank buildings around Donegall Square all sacrificed style to size.

Belfast's centrepiece, the new City Hall, was built on the site of the White Linen Hall by H. & J. Martin at a cost of £360,000 between 1896 and 1906. Complaints of extravagance were partly countered by the Corporation's expenditure on improvements – such as the trams, slum clearance and the new water system – made possible by increased revenue from the burgeoning population. Indeed, the increased strain put on Belfast's infrastructure by its growth was one of the main reasons action had to be taken.

Although Belfast's death rate was now no higher than that in Liverpool or Manchester, public health remained contentious because the annual death rate from tuberculosis was more than double that in England and Wales. By contrast, Purdysburn Fever Hospital, opened by the Corporation's Health Committee in 1906, soon reported that typhoid had been almost eliminated. The General Hospital had evolved into the Royal Victoria Hospital by 1899, and the Corporation donated a site on the Grosvenor Road for a new building which was financed by local donations. Similar philanthropy allowed the Mater Infirmorum Hospital (1883) to be re-developed by 1900. Public and private initiative had helped to ease Belfast's growing pains so that the city's levels of deprivation and squalor were now comparable to those recorded in other British cities.

In 1899 Harland & Wolff launched the world's largest ship, *Oceanic* II, and as the twentieth century began it was indisputably the greatest shipbuilding firm in the world; Workman Clark had also grown in both output and reputation. In 1908 Cunard responded by launching

Edwardian Belfast: the view along Donegall Place to the new City Hall, which was opened on 1 August 1906
DAVID BURNETT

Harland & Wolff, 1911: the *Titanic* nears completion in the background.
HARLAND & WOLFF COLLECTION: UFTM

the *Lusitania* and *Mauretania*, the world's largest and fastest vessels; Harland & Wolff countered with the *Olympic* in 1910, which combined power with passenger comfort. The Harbour Commissioners continued to improve the port's facilities, opening the Musgrave Channel in 1903 and in 1911 opening the Thompson graving dock and deepening the Victoria Channel. As the *Olympic* sailed for Southampton in 1911 her sister ship, the even larger *Titanic*, was launched. On her maiden voyage across the Atlantic, the *Titanic* hit an iceberg and sank on 14 April 1912. Only 711 of the 2,201 passengers survived. News of the disaster stunned the Belfast public, who had expected the front pages of their newspapers to be dominated by the parliamentary debates on the Third Home Rule Bill, for the issue of Irish self-government had re-emerged.

Following the 1906 general election, the new Liberal government's large majority had allowed it to ignore Nationalist demands for Home Rule, but at the 1910 general elections the Liberals and Unionists emerged with almost equal numbers of seats. Nationalists supported the Liberals in return for a new Home Rule Bill, and by August 1911 the powers of the House of Lords had been curtailed so that it could only delay bills from the Commons for two years. Irish unionists could no longer rely on the Commons and Lords to defeat Home Rule as they had done in 1886 and 1893 respectively: the self-reliance shown at the 1892 Ulster Unionist Convention remained their last hope and would now be tested.

The damage to Irish Unionist Party support inflicted by Sloan and Walker in Belfast had been repeated in rural Ulster by the party's fiercest critic, T. W. Russell, whose supporters won two by-elections in 1902 and 1903. Irish Unionist MPs could not repudiate the accusation that they were a clique only concerned with the interests of Protestant landlords and employers and the party leadership in London, and not with those of the Protestant masses. In 1904 Arthur Balfour's Unionist government became associated with a proposal from southern Irish Unionists to grant devolved government to Ireland: Ulster Unionist MPs denounced this as 'Home Rule on the sly' and took the opportunity to distance themselves from the party leadership and to re-establish good relations with their constituents. The Ulster Unionist Council formed in 1905 helped to make constituency associations more representative; the much-maligned Belfast organisation, for example, was refashioned into four constituency associations in 1909. This more populist Ulster Unionist Party, plus the threat of Home Rule from the Liberal government, realigned the Protestant consensus and destroyed independents like Sloan, Walker and Russell. More important, it made possible the creation of a mass movement to resist Home Rule.

'Belfast under Home Rule': Unionist propaganda postcard encapsulating the fears of economic ruin and religious persecution
DAVID BURNETT

The first major public demonstration against Home Rule was in June 1911, when 50,000 men from Orange lodges and the Unionist Clubs assembled at Craigavon, the home of Sir James Craig MP, in east Belfast. Here, the Irish Unionist leader Sir Edward Carson declared, 'We must be prepared the morning Home Rule passes, ourselves to become responsible for the government of the Protestant Province of Ulster.' Home Rulers derided Unionists' talk of a provisional government as a bluff generated by the Protestant landlord elite. However, when Winston Churchill visited Belfast in February 1912 to speak for Home Rule, he was greeted by huge crowds singing 'God Save the King'. At the core of the Unionist campaign were businessmen, professionals and the working classes, and nowhere more so than in Belfast, a city that had prospered under the Union and which feared that a Dublin parliament would impose hurtful tariffs and take Ireland out of the Empire. Protestants also feared Catholic ascendancy: in March 1912 the *Catholic Bulletin* declared that 'To bring into the bosom of Holy Church the million of our separated brethren is a most attractive programme.'

On Easter Tuesday, 1912, Andrew Bonar Law, the Conservative Party leader, was given a magnificent reception at a meeting of 100,000 unionists at Balmoral in south Belfast. In July he declared that if the government did not hold an election, 'I can imagine no length of resistance to which Ulster can go in which I shall not be prepared to support them.' This support was conditional, however: if the Liberals held an election, Bonar Law would abide by the result. The squads of men drilling throughout Ulster showed that unionists there would not accept Home Rule under any circumstances.

Ulster unionists held a series of huge public demonstrations which climaxed in Belfast on 25 September with the signing of the Solemn League and Covenant. That day the city's factories and shops were silent as thousands attended church services in the morning and a monster demonstration outside the City Hall. Here Carson was the first to sign the Covenant that pledged unionists 'to stand by one another in defending for ourselves and our children our cherished position of equal citizenship in the United Kingdom and in using all means which may be found necessary to defeat the present conspiracy to set up a Home Rule Parliament in Ireland'. When the leaders emerged, the vast throng in Donegall Square, Donegall Place and Royal Avenue sang the national anthem and then proceeded to sign the Covenant. J. L. Garvin, a journalist with Home Rule sympathies, no longer believed that Ulster unionists were bluffing: 'no-one for a moment could have mistaken the concentrated will and courage of those people. They do not know what fear and flinching mean in this business, and they are not going to know.'

The aim of the Ulster Unionist leaders was to convince the British public of unionists' determination to resist Home Rule so that pressure would be put on the government to drop or amend the bill: the threat of conflict would prevent civil war. When the government held firm, Carson organised the men who had been drilling into a single body, the Ulster Volunteer Force (UVF), with headquarters at the Old Town Hall in Victoria Street. Escalating military activity would either persuade the government to accept Unionist demands or provide an army for a provisional Unionist government. A war of nerves developed throughout 1913, with each side trying to force the other into a rash action that would cast it in the role of aggressor and forfeit public support. The UVF grassroots wanted to be fully armed, whilst government supporters wanted the Ulster 'rebels' to be faced down.

By spring 1914 both sides had rejected the compromises on offer, which had centred around excluding Ulster or some of the Ulster counties from Home Rule. The government prepared to move troops north and sent ships to Belfast Lough, probably trying to provoke UVF indiscipline, such as attacks on innocent Catholics, which would create a pretext for using the army to break up the UVF's entire structure. Belfast Volunteers were reorganised so that each of the four regiments had a Special Service section of disciplined men ready for any emergency. The refusal of army officers stationed at the Curragh to go to Ulster undermined the government's strategy. Only weeks later Major Fred Crawford from Belfast landed a huge cargo of arms for the UVF at

The 36th (Ulster) Division parades past the City Hall in May 1915. Fourteen months later thousands of these volunteers died at the Somme.
HOGG COLLECTION: ULSTER MUSEUM

Larne. Although this placated UVF militants, it also increased the danger of individual indiscipline and a loss of public sympathy. Nationalists also began to organise a private army, and Belfast Catholics were among the earliest and most enthusiastic recruits. The risk of communal conflict was high.

When war broke out in Europe at the beginning of August 1914, both the Unionist and Nationalist leaderships quickly handed control of their volunteer organisations to the War Office, thus averting a civil war in Ulster which no one wanted. Home Rule was put on the statute book, but implementation was postponed until the cessation of hostilities: special arrangements were to be negotiated for Ulster. Meanwhile Belfast's factories strove to meet the insatiable demands of the British war economy. Harland & Wolff's workforce rose from 15,000 to 20,000, whilst linen exports grew to £20 million in 1916. The port was choked with foodstuffs, textiles, livestock and ores. Wartime inflation, however, ensured that workers were only able to maintain their living standards by working longer hours to earn overtime pay. For thousands of others serving at the front, there were more pressing concerns.

The 36th (Ulster) Division, as the UVF had become in 1914, paraded through Belfast on 8 May 1915 to cheering crowds. On 1 July 1916 the division was at Thiepval Wood ready to go over the top in the Battle of the Somme. Fighting with a remarkable courage, which brought four posthumous Victoria Crosses, the Ulstermen advanced with such astonishing speed that they outran the artillery and were forced to retreat that night.

An English officer who had witnessed the attack, which cost the Ulster Division 5,500 men dead and wounded, wrote:

> I am not an Ulsterman, but yesterday, the 1st of July, as I followed their amazing attack, I felt that I would rather be an Ulsterman than anything else in the world.... Their devotion deserves the gratitude of the British Empire.

At noon on 12 July 1916 Belfast came to a halt as the Somme was remembered. For the families of the many Catholics who had enlisted and died the grief was no less. Nevertheless, the shared experience of sacrifice did not heal the city's political divisions. Ten years earlier Ulster had provided the dormant republican movement with new young leaders such as Denis·McCullough and the Protestant Bulmer Hobson. In 1907 they had helped form Sinn Féin and from Belfast published a weekly paper, the *Republic*. By 1914 the Ulster militants controlled the Irish Republican Brotherhood (IRB), a secret organisation dedicated to revolution to overthrow British government in Ireland: seeing the war as England's difficulty and Ireland's opportunity, they launched a rebellion in Dublin at Easter 1916. Although it was easily defeated, the rebellion polarised political opinion: nationalists increasingly favoured total separation from Britain, and Ulster Unionists were increasingly determined that Ulster, or at least the six north-eastern counties of Ulster, would remain in the UK. Southern unionists and supporters of the old Nationalist Party who sought a compromise on the basis of Home Rule within the Empire were few in number by comparison.

In the general election of 1918, held only weeks after the end of the war, tens of thousands of unskilled workers and women over 30 voted for the first time thanks to the Representation of the People Act (1918) which had more than doubled the Irish electorate. In the country as a whole, Sinn Féin swept aside the old Nationalist Party, winning 73 of the 105 seats and leaving Joe Devlin in West Belfast as the leader of a small rump of six Nationalist MPs. Ulster Unionists increased their representation, from 18 to 26 seats, and in Belfast Carson was elected for the Duncairn division. Carson had been instrumental in forming the Ulster Unionist Labour Association (UULA) in 1917–18 to give Protestant workers a voice in the UUC, telling the shipwrights, 'But for the efforts you made we should never have won [the war] and now that we have we ought to be grateful.' Three UULA MPs were returned in Belfast. Carson's strategy of a Protestant class consensus on the Union, an alternative Ulster democracy to Sinn Féin's Irish democracy, had been realised.

After the war skilled workers in the shipyards wanted improvements in pay and conditions to restore pre-war differentials between themselves and unskilled labourers, whose income had risen during 1916–18. When their union only secured a 47-hour working week and not the 44-hour week they had demanded, the shipyard men and other skilled workers went on strike in January 1919. Unionist politicians were instinctively hostile, but they were reluctant to alienate workers who had voted for them and served with them in the UVF or the Ulster Division, and therefore they did little. Devlin, however, demanded military intervention to smash the strike, and troops were transferred north to occupy gasworks and electricity stations. This enabled civilians to work the plants, and by 19 February the strike had collapsed.

The Protestant strikers resented the lack of support from the Ulster Unionist Party so soon after the general election. At the Corporation election of January 1920, which was was fought under proportional representation, they took revenge and Ulster Unionists were reduced from 52 to 29 councillors. Official Labour Unionists won 6 seats, the Belfast Labour Party won 10 and independent Labour candidates 3; 10 of the councillors were trade unionists. Protestant voting for labour parties was not a dilution of their unionism but an effort to gain socio-economic improvements and to increase working-class influence within the Protestant class consensus.

In 1919 Sinn Féin had established its own parliament, Dáil Éireann, and the Irish Volunteers, soon to be known as the Irish Republican Army (IRA), launched a guerrilla war against the government. By mid-1920 the Anglo-Irish War reached rural Ulster. During 1914–18 many Catholics had been able to enter what had been exclusively Protestant trades in Belfast and Protestant workers resented this economic threat. The IRA campaign heightened Protestant fears that the influx of Catholic workers was part of the Sinn Féin campaign to take control of Ireland. Protestant workers responded by driving an estimated 11,000 Catholics and Protestant socialists from the shipyards, Barbours, Musgraves, Mackies and the Sirocco Works. Rioting ensued, and by the end of August twenty-two people were dead. A military curfew was imposed on Belfast until 1924: everyone was required to 'remain indoors between the hours of 10.30 p.m. and 5 a.m.' Nevertheless, by the end of 1920, seventy-four people had been killed.

Since 1916, Ulster Unionist leaders had been negotiating the details of Ulster's future with the coalition government of Liberals and Unionists. By 1920 it had been agreed that six counties of Ulster would become Northern Ireland with a parliament at Belfast. Ulster Unionist leaders were anxious to have the Government of Ireland Act implemented quickly as 'without a parliament of our own ... constant attempts would be made ... to draw us into a Dublin parliament'. Moreover, a Belfast parliament would provide loyalists with the legal authority to take on the IRA.

6
CAPITAL CITY
1921–72

King George V opens the new Northern Ireland parliament in Belfast City Hall, 22 June 1921.
ULSTER MUSEUM

On 3 May 1921 Belfast officially became the capital of Northern Ireland. James Craig, the new Ulster Unionist leader, became prime minister after a resounding victory at the first elections to the new parliament on 24 May: fifteen Unionists and one Nationalist, the party leader Joe Devlin, were returned in Belfast. Sinn Féin's aim had been 'to smash the Ulster Parliament' and having failed at this election it would 'have to be smashed otherwise'. IRA attacks had been ongoing since 1920 and a Special Constabulary, drawn heavily from the old UVF, had been formed in response. In effect the communal rioting of the past had been institutionalised, with firearms augmenting stones and cudgels. On

22 June, King George V opened the Northern Ireland parliament at Belfast City Hall and appealed for a truce between the IRA and Crown forces. On 11 July, following weeks of gun battles, evictions and the destruction of houses in Belfast, such a truce was agreed.

But Belfast benefited little from it. Craig accepted that David Lloyd George and Eamon de Valera could negotiate arrangements between London and Dublin so long as Northern Ireland was left alone, but both Lloyd George and de Valera saw Northern Ireland as a bargaining chip. Lloyd George pressed Craig to make concessions while Belfast goods were boycotted by the Dáil, leaving loyalists feeling isolated and betrayed. In Belfast sectarian riots continued, resulting in many deaths. Craig's resolution forced Lloyd George and the majority in Sinn Féin to agree to a settlement that left Northern Ireland's future to be decided by a boundary commission. Thus Unionist insecurity remained, whilst northern Nationalists could hope that a policy of abstention, whereby they refused to recognise or co-operate with the Northern Ireland government and institutions, would undermine the state.

The IRA launched a major offensive against Northern Ireland in January 1922. In Belfast 31 people were killed between 12 and 16 February: in March 61 people died. Indiscriminate bombings, house burnings and barbarous sectarian assassinations intensified divisions within the city. In April the Royal Ulster Constabulary (RUC) of 50,000 regular and part-time constables was established and the Civil Authorities (Special Powers) Bill was enacted: neither a massive police presence nor the draconian emergency powers of the new act prevented the deaths of 36 people that month. W. J. Twaddell, Unionist MP for West Belfast, was among the 66 people killed in May. A combination of stern government action and IRA withdrawal to the south, where the civil war was beginning, gave Belfast a comparatively peaceful summer. Sixteen Catholics were killed in the second half of the year but the arrest of their Ulster Protestant Association murderers brought almost total peace by the beginning of 1923. However, the death toll of over 450 since July 1920 pointed to a difficult future.

The decline of Belfast's staple industries – shipbuilding, textiles and engineering – ensured that unemployment rates hovered around 20 per cent throughout the 1920s, adding economic misery to political uncertainty. These established industries tried to sell goods of which there was a surplus abroad, a difficulty compounded by Britain's return to the Gold Standard in 1925 which overpriced British goods abroad: the numbers of those employed in linen fell from 86,762 in 1924 to 70,421 in 1925. New industries such as chemicals and motor car manufacture did not come to Belfast, which became the centre of the most disadvantaged industrial area in the UK.

In Britain in the same period the Labour Party grew. In Belfast, however, the labour movement could not compete with the sectarian animosity aroused between 1920 and 1922. When Craig's government abolished proportional representation (PR) for local elections in June 1922, the main losers in Belfast were not the Nationalists, who gained two seats, but the Labour parties: Protestant workers voted Unionist to avoid splitting the anti-Nationalist vote. The City Hall Unionist Party, which would have won under any democratic electoral system, was characterised as a 'fur coat brigade' representing the prosperous business and professional classes, but its members did show some constructive enterprise. The Harbour Power Station was opened in 1923, the UK's first municipal aerodrome opened at Malone in 1924, and the Gas Department was so efficient that it could supply cheap gas and make enough profit to subsidise the rates, electricity, libraries, parks and public baths. Over £3 million was spent on street widening and bridge building in the 1920s, but keeping the rates low was the city fathers' priority, and public health and housing remained neglected.

Similar complacency affected Belfast's education system, and a report of 1922 estimated that 12,000 local children were without school accommodation. Lord Londonderry's Education Act (1923) envisaged striking improvements by increasing grants and making local authorities responsible for schools. The Belfast Education Committee showed real initiative, closing down dilapidated schools and building impressive new schools such as Euston Street, Mountcollyer and Mersey Street. School meals were served from 1926 to needy children. Secondary education did not see the rapid expansion of grammar school places for able working-class children as in Britain, but there were notable successes such as J. C. Beckett and T. W. Moody who both became renowned professors of Irish history.

Though Londonderry's Education Act did not allow religious instruction during school hours in state schools, Catholic school managers would not transfer their buildings to the control of the Belfast Education Committee, preferring a system 'wherein Catholic children are taught in Catholic schools by Catholic teachers'. Abstention by Nationalist MPs, clergy and educationalists meant that the new state's education policy was framed without Catholic input and their schools emerged worse off: the government paid teachers' salaries but only 50 per cent of maintenance costs and nothing towards building costs. When Christian Brothers schools in Belfast accepted some state control in 1926, they gained an additional £10,000 a year.

Education became a battlefield in the 1930s: the United Education Committee of the Protestant Churches campaigned for Bible instruction in classes and clerical representation on management committees; the Catholic bishops sought improved funding. Craig capitulated to Protestant demands in 1925 and 1930, and Catholics were placated by 50 per cent grants for school building and improvements; four new Catholic schools were subsequently opened in 1932. Teacher training was also segregated by religion: Catholics trained at St Mary's College and Protestants at Stranmillis College, which opened in 1929; the government paid for both. A shilling rate designated for education allowed unsuitable schools to be closed or renovated and new schools, including Strandtown, Edenvale, Seaview and Botanic, to be built in Belfast throughout the decade.

The Corporation's Housing Committee was loath to accept that under the Wheatley Housing Act (1924) it had a responsibility to build houses at affordable rents. Between 1923 and 1936 the Corporation helped to amend Northern Ireland housing legislation to ensure that private enterprise combined with public subsidy remained the norm. Not only did this system lead to corruption and abuse, but the houses built were often beyond the means of the working class. Hundreds of kitchen and parlour houses were built under the Subsidy Scheme at Whiterock, Donegall Avenue and Seaview; at Ulsterville, Woodvale, Stranmillis, Donegall Road and Skegoniel as part of a Corporation public works scheme; and at Wandsworth, Cherryvalley, Dundela and Rosebery Road under the Assisted Scheme. The Housing Committee refused to subsidise rents to a lower level because, as one government minister put it in 1932, 'builders are not philanthropists'. Between the First and Second World Wars, 34,312 houses were built in Northern Ireland, but Belfast Corporation was directly responsible for only 2,600.

Poor housing, low incomes and high unemployment hindered efforts to improve public health in a city with high death and infant mortality rates. The need for improvements was recognised in 1927 but the government, struggling to pay unemployment benefits, did not have the money to implement them. It was left to Belfast's Public Health Department to provide noble but amateurish controls on food, milk, abattoirs and ships coming into port. The Corporation would not raise rates to pay for a more professional service. Neighbouring local authorities such as Carrickfergus and Holywood could negate Belfast's good work by allowing untreated sewage into Belfast Lough, and infected animals were regularly brought to Belfast abattoirs from the countryside. By contrast, the expanding Royal Victoria Hospital, the new Royal and Jubilee maternity hospitals, and the Purdysburn institution for the mentally ill provided improvements in health care. And the Silent Valley reservoir was a superb engineering feat, storing enough Mourne water to provide a further 11 million gallons a day to Belfast.

Belfast did not join the General Strike of 1926 but as unemployment persisted, unrest grew. The main target for criticism was the Board of Guardians (responsible for aiding the destitute whose unemployment insurance had been exhausted), who believed their 'duty was to discourage idleness and to create a spirit of independence since much of the money given to the poor is wasted'. Belfast MPs representing both communities, such as Jack Beattie, Joe Devlin, Tommy Henderson, William McMullan and Sam Kyle, united in their criticism. When the government refused to compel the Board of Guardians to expand outdoor relief, that is, to provide food and clothing as an alternative to the workhouse, an exasperated J. H. Andrews wrote to Lord Craigavon (as Craig had become in 1927): 'How they can call themselves the guardians of the poor I do not know as they approach the whole problem from the one viewpoint alone, namely, saving the ratepayers.'

Charities provided alternative relief; the St Vincent de Paul Society, for example, spent £12,150 a year and helped twelve times as many as the Board of Guardians. This could never be enough, however, and the government at last passed legislation that increased outdoor relief though this was far short of reforms in Britain where the Poor Law was replaced by doles; that is, unemployment payments as of right; moreover, the Belfast Guardians were slow to implement the changes. Lying somewhere between unemployment payments and the desire 'to cut off grants to parasites', the new legislation provided grocery chits for work done on public schemes such as road resurfacing.

The Great Depression of 1929–31 affected Belfast for a decade. By December 1932 unemployment in shipbuilding and engineering was 64.5 per cent: Harland & Wolff did not launch a single ship in 1932 or 1933, whilst Workman Clark's lack of orders forced it to close in 1935. Linen was priced out of the international market by cotton and rayon, and the numbers employed in the industry fell from 86,762 in 1924 to

61,000 in 1935. The situation was desperate: a man arrested for breaking shop windows explained, 'I broke the windows because I was hungry. Jail is the only place where I can get food.'

The opening of the new Northern Ireland parliament building, Stormont, a fine neoclassical structure in magnificent grounds in east Belfast, in November 1932, stood in marked contrast. At the close of parliamentary sittings in the City Hall the previous September, Craig had risen to speak, only to be interrupted by Jack Beattie and Tommy Henderson, Labour and Unionist MPs for Pottinger and Shankill respectively. Henderson poured a torrent of invective at the ministerial benches:

> We have not met for four months and we are going to adjourn for another two months; in the meantime the starving people of Northern Ireland are to continue starving. . . . What about the 78,000 who are starving?

The number of people 'out of benefit', that is no longer eligible for cash payments because their unemployment insurance was exhausted and thus reliant upon outdoor relief, had been rising alarmingly. Moreover, the outdoor relief was inadequate. Hunger and destitution brought 60,000 Protestants and Catholics together on 3 October 1932 for a torchlit rally outside the Custom House. Two days later, with no new help in sight, the desperate were rioting.

After a week of disturbances the Unemployed Workers' Committee planned a march for 11 October. This was banned by the government and when the marchers were met by police, conflict erupted in the Albert Street area of the Falls. J. J. Kelly recalled a woman announcing the news to crowds on the Shankill Road and asking, 'Are youse goin' to let them down?', to which they replied, 'No, by heavens we are not.' The trouble spread to the York Street and Newtownards Road areas and grew in ferocity, forcing the government and Corporation to coerce the Board of Guardians into increasing relief payments.

Even in the depths of recession, however, the majority of insured workers in Belfast remained in employment. Companies such as Gallahers and Davidson's Sirocco Works increased production or continued to dominate international markets. Linen remained the city's biggest employer, the low wages and harsh conditions offset by regular pay and camaraderie. The employed could not only buy cheap food but could enjoy dances at ballrooms such as the Orpheus and the new talkies at the growing number of cinemas.

In these years of uncertainty and decline Belfast shook off its reputation as a cultural wasteland. John Lavery was the first Belfast man to win international fame as

Cross-channel steamers at Donegall Quay, 17 August 1929. So many people from Britain wanted to attend the Tourist Trophy motorcycle race on the Newtownards circuit that extra ships had to be laid on at Liverpool and Heysham.
BELFAST HARBOUR COMMISSIONERS

an artist, and William Conor's lively street scenes provide an undervalued record of the inter-war city. The writer C. S. Lewis was born at 47 Dundela Avenue but it was the city's finest poet, Louis MacNeice (1907–63), who captured its character best:

> See Belfast, devout and profane and hard,
> Built on reclaimed mud, hammers playing in the
>   shipyard
> Time punched with holes like a steel sheet, time
> Hardening the faces, veneering with a grey and speckled
>   rime
> The faces under the shawls and caps:
> This was my mother-city, these my paps.

The solidarity of Catholic and Protestant workers in 1932 allowed Harry Midgley, a Protestant and a known critic of clericalism, and Jack Beattie, a Protestant anti-partitionist, to win Dock and Pottinger for Labour in the 1933 Stormont election. However, the unrelenting slump caused by the Depression placed Protestants and Catholics in direct competition for jobs and helped preserve traditional sectarian tensions. Craigavon's declaration in 1934 that Stormont was a 'Protestant Parliament for a Protestant People', drew fierce criticism from loyalists who believed his government was not living up to the claim. A ban imposed on all parades in mid-1935, following riots in east Belfast, would have affected the Orange demonstrations on the Twelfth of July but the ban was lifted in response to backbench pressure. At the Belfast Twelfth celebrations, Sir Joseph Davison, the Orange Grand Master, explained loyalist fears of nationalist empowerment: 'the aim of these people is to establish an all-Ireland Roman Catholic State, in which Protestantism will be crushed out of existence'.

As the Orangemen returned to the city, a minor scuffle near Lancaster Street provided the spark for full-scale confrontation between Catholic and Protestant mobs, leading to 'the worst night of disorder since 1920–22'. Two civilians were killed, 35 civilians and 3 policemen were wounded, 14 houses were set on fire and 47 other dwellings were wrecked. Police and troops could not enforce a curfew and despite efforts by the clergy to restore peace the rioting continued. By the end of August, 13 people had been killed and hundreds of families, mostly Catholics, had been driven from their homes.

Sectarian rivalry over jobs had been intensified by the deterioration of north–south relations. Since 1932, de Valera's Free State government had been waging an 'economic war' with Britain, damaging Belfast's southern trade. Then, in 1937, a bolder Catholic–Gaelic nationalism was enshrined in the constitution. As this laid claim to Northern Ireland, Craigavon called an election early in 1938 to reaffirm the Union. This response convinced the unionist electorate that the Ulster Unionist Party could be trusted and ensured that militant loyalist alternatives such as the Progressive Unionist Party were defeated. In contrast, the Labour and anti-Union votes suffered serious divisions. Midgley's meetings were broken up by supporters of his Nationalist opponent, James Collins, who in turn had his meetings attacked by republicans. The Ulster Unionists won Midgley's Dock seat, leaving Jack Beattie, who had been expelled from the Belfast Labour Party for his anti-partitionist views, as the city's sole Labour MP. Craigavon was 'the only politician who can win an election without leaving his fireside', the *Daily Express* commented.

The threat of war in Europe prompted British

Stirling bombers being manufactured at Short & Harland, January 1941
SHORTS PLC

rearmament at the end of 1935, and in 1936 Belfast was chosen as a major centre for aircraft production. Parliamentary permission to build an aerodrome at Sydenham had already been obtained by the Harbour Commissioners; Short Brothers of Rochester, backed by government money, joined with Harland & Wolff to begin aircraft production on the nearby Queen's Island. By the end of 1937, 6,000 people were on Short & Harland's payroll, building Bristol Bombay transporters and Hereford bombers. Delivery was slow at first but the outbreak of war in September 1939 forced production to increase and soon the company was also producing the RAF's first heavy bomber, the Stirling, and the Sunderland flying boat. Harland & Wolff built the cruiser HMS *Belfast*, the aircraft carrier HMS *Formidable*, and numerous smaller vessels for the Royal Navy. James Mackie & Sons produced shells, and the Sirocco Works made ventilators for munitions stores. With Westminster promising to reform financial arrangements with Stormont to Northern Ireland's benefit, as well as providing millions of pounds' worth of contracts, Belfast's economy seemed set for recovery.

However, the dislocation caused by the transfer to wartime production and shortages of raw materials hampered efforts to mobilise the labour force, and unemployment rose every month until February 1940.

Initial enthusiasm for air-raid defences and shelters, the evacuation of children and a comprehensive black-out soon evaporated. Both government and public began to believe that Belfast was out of range of German bombers, and materials to build shelters and provide adequate fire-fighting equipment were not requisitioned. Craigavon's priority was for Northern Ireland to prove its loyalty to King and country: he declared, 'We are King's Men and we shall be with you to the end', in a radio broadcast to Britain in early 1940. After Dunkirk, Belfast found itself playing a crucial role in combating German U-boats in the Western Approaches: Churchill wrote, 'Here by the Grace of God, Ulster stood a faithful sentinel.' Craigavon also concentrated on destroying a small IRA 'fifth column' which was trying to rekindle the spirit of 1916 by helping Germany. All the while, Belfast remained unprotected from air attack: by March 1941 anti-aircraft cover was less than half the approved strength and there were no searchlights. Craigavon died in November 1940, and John Andrews, the new prime minister, knew that a raid was probable in early April 1941, but there was little he could now do to prepare the city.

On the night of 7–8 April, six German bombers raided the Docks area, destroying Harland & Wolff's fuselage factory. A week later, on 15 April, some 200 Junkers, Heinkels and Dorniers devastated Belfast, killing more than 700 people, wounding 1,500, destroying 1,600 homes, and damaging 28,000 more. Before defences could be strengthened, the Luftwaffe returned

Belfast families search wreckage after the Blitz on Easter Tuesday,
15–16 April 1941.

on 4–5 May. Thousands of civilians had fled to provincial towns or were sleeping rough in the countryside and the main targets were industrial, but still 150 people were killed and 157 were badly injured. Ships were sunk and the Harbour Power Station and York Street railway station were destroyed. Shipping construction fell by 45 per cent and took six months to recover. Stirling bomber production was seriously delayed. Around 15,000 citizens were homeless, 40,000 were in rest centres, and 70,000 were receiving meals in emergency centres. 'New friendships were forged ... kindness and a helping hand appeared from the most unexpected quarters,' Jim McConville recalled, but public disaffection with the inept government and Corporation was strong.

Hungry children lined up to be deloused and adults, made unemployed by the destruction of industry, joined the food queues. Stormont took over the affairs of the Corporation, including the setting of rates and the allocation of contracts, for three and a half years. This did not save the government from unpopularity and the Labour candidate Midgley took the safe Unionist seat of Willowfield at a by-election in December 1941. Andrews became increasingly unpopular and in April 1943 he was forced by his own colleagues to resign.

Sir Basil Brooke, who had led the cabinet revolt, became prime minister at a time when the economy was recovering. The Harland & Wolff workforce grew from 9,100 to 20,600 between 1939 and 1945, enabling the company to complete 150 ships, 10,000 field guns and 550 tanks; the Sirocco Works and Mackies produced grenades, radar equipment and shells; whilst the 100,000 US troops in Northern Ireland by the end of 1943 spent money freely in the shops, restaurants, cinemas and theatres. Shorts produced over 1,000 aircraft, the 865 Stirlings reaping a terrible revenge on German cities. Although unemployment rarely fell below 15,000 between 1942 and 1944, Belfast had never seen such prosperity. Income levels in 1939 had been about half those in Britain, but by 1945 they stood at three-quarters of the greatly increased income levels in Britain. With the IRA once again inoperative and sectarian animosity reduced by common experience and general prosperity, Belfast seemed to have been saved by the war.

The post-war victory enjoyed in Britain by Clement Attlee's Labour Party had a milder resonance in Belfast. At the Stormont elections of June 1945 the Ulster Unionists confirmed their primacy, but Labour candidates did well in Belfast considering that the different Labour parties, divided by religion and the constitutional question, split each other's votes in several constituencies: independents like Beattie and Midgley won Pottinger and Willowfield, the Labour Party won Dock, Oldpark and, in 1946, Central, whilst Tommy Henderson, the Independent Unionist MP for Shankill, was as much a Labour MP as these. In the Westminster election Beattie took West Belfast again, and in the Corporation elections of 1946 the Labour Party increased its representation from four to eight councillors. The basis of Labour's success was the Beveridge proposals of 1942 for a welfare state.

Unionist MPs at Westminster had opposed the various welfare measures approved by parliament, but Unionist attitudes changed shortly afterwards and the measures were enacted by Stormont with much enthusiasm. The explanation for this lay in Westminster's preparedness to pay most of the very large sum needed to finance welfarism in Northern Ireland. In 1946 it was agreed that, provided parity of taxation was maintained, Northern Ireland would enjoy the same standard of services as the rest of the UK: welfare needs were greater in Northern Ireland, but it would receive enough funds to allow it to catch up with Britain.

Housing was a priority, since the Blitz had destroyed 3,200 homes and damaged 53,000, and thousands more were unfit for habitation or overcrowded. These problems were acute in the inner city. The Housing Trust was established with power to borrow from the Stormont government to build houses. It had to pay its own way, however, and fix rents in relation to construction costs. This ensured that it could not supply cheap housing for those most in need, though the new estates it built at Cregagh, Andersonstown and Finaghy provided some relief. Stormont and Corporation schemes, such as subsidising private builders and prefabricated bungalows, augmented the trust's work, and by 1954, 11,000 houses had been erected. Nevertheless thousands of applicants remained on the housing waiting list and slum housing had not been tackled comprehensively.

The Blitz had once again highlighted the city's low standards of health care and now prompted government action. Tuberculosis was the main killer and the Tuberculosis Authority, established in 1941 to extirpate the disease, had by 1954 reduced the death rate to around the British average. Brooke established a new Ministry of Health and Local Government in 1944, with William Grant, a former shipyard worker, as minister; this helped to prepare the way for the National Health Service in 1948. Belfast's chaotic, overlapping network of dispensary system, separate hospital administrations and Poor Law was replaced by the Northern Ireland General Health Services Board and the Hospitals Board. The workhouse became Belfast City Hospital; a central laboratory, a radiotherapy centre and a blood transfusion service were established in Belfast; Wakehurst House, with 200 geriatric beds, was built; outpatient departments increased from 46 to 85; chairs in Dentistry and Mental Health were established at Queen's; an experimental ward unit opened at Musgrave Park; and an Institute of Clinical Science serviced the teaching hospitals. In Belfast deaths in childbirth fell to British levels by 1954, and by the 1960s mortality rates in Northern Ireland as a whole were the lowest in Britain and Ireland.

Belfast's education system had been seriously disrupted by the Blitz: 18 schools had been destroyed and 34 damaged. Nevertheless education's reputation grew during the war: teachers maintained a school system of sorts, and organised the evacuation of children and the billeting of the homeless; the Corporation's Education

Committee under Dr Stuart Hawnt introduced school meals and milk; the number of grammar school scholarships rose from 50 to 200; and Grosvenor High School was opened. More important, the Education Act passed by the Westminster parliament in 1944, which in Britain provided for primary education to age eleven and for free and compulsory secondary education within a system of grammar, secondary and technical schools, was accepted by Stormont.

In both health and education, however, sectarianism coloured the reforms. The 1947 Health Act operating in Britain allowed denominational hospitals to retain their religious character, but the Northern Ireland variation omitted this: the Mater Hospital, although open to anyone, was a Catholic foundation and refused to come under the Hospitals Authority, a refusal that damaged its funding. The Catholic bishops and Nationalist leaders claimed that the new legislation would 'establish a colossal system of state controlled education': proposals to increase capital grants from 50 to 65 per cent, to provide milk and meals for necessitous children and books free of charge were interpreted as pressure to join the state system. However, opposition to the bill came also from Protestant traditionalists who objected to its non-denominational character and accused Stormont ministers of 'a betrayal of Protestantism'. Although the bill became law in 1947, Harry Midgley's defection to the Unionist Party in 1947 in support of the traditionalists demonstrated that despite the shared experience of war, Belfast's sectarianism was alive and well.

Thus the Corporation's Education Committee divided Belfast into twelve districts, and Catholic managers grouped their parishes into five areas to implement the new act's nursery, primary and secondary provisions. There were insufficient secondary school places, however, and elementary schools such as Eden-derry, Glenwood, Lichfield Park and Park Parade were hurriedly converted: purpose-built secondary schools appeared throughout the 1950s, with, for example, Ballygomartin Boys', Everton Boys' and Orangefield Boys' schools opening in 1957–58. Initially, Grosvenor was the Education Committee's only grammar school, as the established grammar schools hovered between independence and direct control by mixing private fees and government grants. By 1959 there were still only three state grammar schools, attended by 1,898 pupils. Not only had sectarian divisions in education been maintained, but, by paying supplementary fees to the established grammar schools Belfast's middle classes had ensured that class barriers would also remain intact. Further education developed at the Stanhope Street Further Education Centre, the Jaffe School, the expand-ing College of Technology, and the Rupert Stanley College, opened in 1965. By then the Belfast Education Committee was spending £3 million a year.

The expansion of higher education drew into the city a talented new generation which enhanced Belfast's reputation in the creative arts. Michael McLaverty's novels portrayed the experiences of rural migrants in Belfast, whilst Sam Hanna Bell, the author of the novel *December Bride*, used the city as a setting for his later fic-tion. Brian Moore, born in Clifton Street, became Belfast's first author to earn a truly international reputa-tion. Unlike earlier writers such as St John Ervine who were proud of Belfast's industrial might, Moore vilified the city for its bleakness, pathetic downtrodden people, inept politicians and suffocating bigotry and sexual prudery. In poetry, John Hewitt managed both to condemn his 'creed-haunted, godforsaken race' and to earn himself a reputation as the authentic voice of Ulster Protestants. At Queen's, Laurence Lerner, Philip Larkin and Philip Hobsbaum inspired young poets like Seamus Heaney whose first collection, *Death of a Naturalist* (1966), won critical acclaim. The Group Theatre produced dozens of plays and helped Joseph Tomelty, Jack Loudan and Gerald McLarnon to establish themselves as playwrights; later it became the 'Home of Ulster Comedy' and of the most versatile caricaturist of the Belfast character, James Young. An alternative stage for local writers was provided by Mary and Pearse O'Malley's small Lyric Theatre. For all this, the controversy surrounding the performance of Sam Thompson's *Over the Bridge*, which dealt with sectarianism in the shipyards, at the Empire in 1960 served as a reminder of the sectarian hatreds lurking below Belfast's surface in these quieter years.

In September 1948 John A. Costello, prime minister in the south of Ireland, had announced that his state would become a republic. Attlee responded that no change would take place in Northern Ireland's constitutional position 'without Northern Ireland's free agreement'. Consequently, Brooke called an election to confirm that Northern Ireland was British. Southern politicians established an anti-partition fund to aid anti-Unionist candidates; as this was collected at Mass, the election was quickly dubbed 'the chapel gate election'. Jack Beattie accepted funds and had his meetings broken up, whilst opposition candidates in Dock and Cromac were stoned. The Unionists eliminated the Northern Ireland Labour Party (NILP), gaining its three Belfast seats; Beattie's defeat in Pottinger left only two anti-partition Labour MPs representing Belfast and meant that for the first time all opposition MPs would be Catholics. The Labour movement could no longer straddle the constitutional question; the NILP declared its unionism and anti-partitionists banded together under the Irish Labour Party.

Throughout the 1950s Harland & Wolff benefited from the post-war reconstruction boom underpinned by Marshall Aid from the USA. As shipping companies strove to replace wartime losses, so Harland & Wolff regularly launched over 100,000 tons a year, making it the largest shipbuilding unit in the world. Few realised, however, that the launch of the liner *Canberra* in 1960 was the end of an era – that air transport would soon eclipse sea travel. Foreign competition and declining maritime freight pushed Harland & Wolff's workforce down from 20,000 to 13,000; even a modernisation programme, which enabled the yard to win contracts for oil tankers, could not prevent the numbers from falling to around 10,000 by 1970. The decline of linen was even more striking. After the Second World War government price controls and high demand allowed the mills to flourish, but a sudden collapse between July 1951 and July 1952 forced two of the biggest mills, York Street and Brookfield, to close. Employment fell by 50 per cent and failed to recover as rayon, cotton and the new synthetics, which could resist modern detergents damaging to linen, captured the market. Most of Ireland's two hundred linen firms had been in Belfast, but by 1980 only twenty remained.

At a time when unemployment in Britain was negligible, Belfast had unemployment rates varying from 10.4 per cent in 1952 to 6.4 per cent in 1956 and 9.3 per cent in 1958. The Belfast area, with 60 per cent of Northern Ireland's industrial workers, was suffering persistent unemployment, especially amongst the unskilled. High costs, inflicted in particular by the dependence on imported coal, and by the need for cross-channel transportation, put Belfast at a disadvantage compared to cities in Britain. Traditionally, employers had compensated by paying lower wages than employers in Britain, but national pay deals were bringing Belfast wages increasingly into line. Economists predicted that Belfast's competitiveness would be reduced. If unemployment was not to grow, output per worker would have to increase or substantial aid would have to be given by the Westminster government.

Almost all the increase in industrial employment between 1948 and the late 1950s was the result of government aid, but still unemployment persisted. In the 1958 Stormont election the NILP questioned the government's commitment to job creation and won four seats in Belfast. Two of these, Woodvale and Victoria, were hitherto safe Unionist seats. Although unwavering in their support for the Union, the four NILP MPs formed an official opposition and criticised government inactivity in promoting economic recovery. In the 1962 election they retained their seats with increased majorities. Criticism from senior civil servants on the Hall Committee and from Desmond Boal, Unionist MP for Shankill, convinced the Unionist Party to dump Lord Brookeborough. His successor as prime minister, Captain Terence O'Neill, declared, 'We have held the line while old industries have faltered. But it is not enough. We must do more. We intend to do more.'

With the old staple industries declining, O'Neill accepted the Wilson Plan of December 1964 which urged a major drive to attract new industry from Britain and abroad. This was to be implemented in conjunction with the Matthew Stop Line which was to mark the limits of Belfast beyond which the city should not grow: a new city, Craigavon, was to be built between Portadown and Lurgan, and seven nearby towns were to become growth centres. The aim was to spread industrial development more widely in Northern Ireland and to induce Belfast residents who could not be properly rehoused within the city after slum clearance to move away. Belfast Corporation was upset that it would be denied rates from prosperous householders and businesses in the fringe area beyond the Stop Line and declared:

> It is optimistic to restrict the one proven growth point in an increasingly competitive world, on the assumption that potential industrial customers can be steered elsewhere for charitable purposes.

When the government pressed ahead, Belfast's redevelopment programme slowed down. Moreover, as people refused to move out of the city the new-

Mill housing in Sandy Row dating from the early to middle nineteenth century, still inhabited in July 1965

Old and new: looking north from Albert Street/Durham Street. In the foreground the Durham Street Weaving Company and the congested housing of the lower Falls; in the background a Liebherr crane stands beside the Divis Flats complex, nearing completion.
LINEN HALL LIBRARY

building areas within the Matthew Stop Line – Benview, Moyard, Turf Lodge and Blackmountain – had to be developed at very high density, thus storing up trouble for the future. Indeed the housing shortage in Belfast became so acute that new estates at Ballybeen, Ballyduff, New Mossley, Glencairn and Twinbrook had to be built in the late 1960s and early 1970s.

The inducements offered to outside companies nevertheless did attract new industry to Northern Ireland, and ultimately they benefited Belfast. The fringe of the city saw the growth of industrial estates where factories were supplemented with housing, shops, recreational facilities, schools and churches: the fall in population between 1951 and 1961, from 443,671 to 416,094, was reflected in the growth in the fringe area from 120,000 in 1951 to 220,000 by 1966. A major factor was the growth in car ownership which, in combination with buses, led to the demise of the tram network. Groups of factories at Castlereagh, Dunmurry, Whitehouse, Carnmoney and Monkstown flanked planned residential areas. Companies such as British Oxygen, BVC, ICI and Hughes Tool Company brought prosperity to Castlereagh, while Autolite and Grundig benefited Dunmurry. Light engineering, liberated by cheaper electricity from the need to be close to coal and the docks, meant around 20,000 new jobs for the Belfast conurbation by 1967.

Some established industries also thrived: James Mackie and Sons manufactured a full range of textile machinery, including a range for the new synthetic fibres, and had around 6,000 employees by the late 1960s. The Sirocco Works continued to produce specialist ventilation equipment for export, whilst the Belfast Ropeworks was the largest cordage factory in the world until its closure in 1966. Shorts grew, thanks to government contracts, the development of innovative aircraft such as the Fokker passenger airliners and the Skyvan light aircraft, and the production of anti-aircraft missiles: by the 1960s the company was the second-biggest employer in Northern Ireland. The growth of service-sector jobs, especially in the public sector where there were 22,000 central and local government officials by 1967, helped to bring unemployment down to around 3 per cent. But Belfast's dependence on prosperous export markets made it vulnerable and when that prosperity evaporated a decade later, much of the economic structure of these years also collapsed.

The appearance of the Rolling Stones at the Ulster Hall in August 1964 to 'almost unbelievable scenes of mass hysteria' made Belfast seem little different from other European cities. An IRA campaign in the 1950s had been unsuccessful and had had scarcely any impact on Belfast; the NILP's electoral success signalled Protestant confidence that the Union was safe. O'Neill even felt able to make friendly gestures towards the Catholic community, recognising the Northern Committee of the Irish Congress of Trade Unions, visiting Catholic schools, and having talks with Cardinal Conway.

Yet underneath the surface the old community tensions remained. During the Westminster election campaign of 1964, police were ordered by the Stormont government to remove an Irish tricolour from a republican election office in Divis Street, and rioting ensued. The disturbances ended quickly and provoked no immediate sequel, however. O'Neill remained determined to continue his détente strategy and took the bold step of inviting the Republic's premier, Sean Lemass, to Belfast. O'Neill's confident unionism, combined with economic reforms, in 1965 allowed the Ulster Unionists to regain Protestant votes and seats lost to the NILP: the NILP had lost Catholic support after the so-called 'Sunday swings' affair, when NILP councillors had

'We both share the same rivers, the same mountains, and some of the same problems': Prime Minister Terence O'Neill (right) greets Taoiseach Sean Lemass at Stormont, 14 January 1965.
PUBLIC RECORD OFFICE OF NORTHERN IRELAND

backed traditional Protestant sabbatarian objections to the plans of the Corporation's Education Committee to open recreational facilities on Sundays.

But O'Neill's strategy alienated militants within his cabinet. And as many Catholics grew impatient for wholesale reforms, many Protestants grew restless lest the constitution should become endangered: the age-old incompatibility between Catholic empowerment and Protestant security became prominent once again. The Reverend Ian Paisley, Moderator of the Free Presbyterian Church, led the protests against ecumenism and the visits of southern politicians. As O'Neill's most strident critic, he attracted support from loyalist workers, especially in east Belfast; they were increasingly disgusted by the prime minister's patrician liberal unionism. In June 1966, following a series of minor incidents, Paisley led a march through Cromac Square in the Catholic Markets area and rioting ensued. Sporadic street violence continued throughout the year, which marked the fiftieth anniversary of both the Easter Rising and the Battle of the Somme; three people were killed in separate incidents by a group calling itself the Ulster Volunteer Force and in December O'Neill declared that the violence had 'disfigured our reputation throughout the English-speaking world'.

In 1967, at the International Hotel in Donegall Square South, the Northern Ireland Civil Rights Association was formed, though the initiative for the movement had come from west of the River Bann and not from Belfast. In Londonderry and several rural councils there was irrefutable evidence that Unionists had manipulated, or gerrymandered, local government boundaries in order to manufacture or safeguard Unioinist majorities, and of favouritism in housing allocation and employment. A fierce debate over how Northern Ireland was governed and how the Catholic minority was treated had begun. The civil rights movement placed unreasonably high hopes for radical change on reforming the local government franchise, whereby only ratepayers could vote, through the introduction of universal suffrage: O'Neill's government held firm. As marches and counter-marches merged into attack, counter-attack, riot and murder, the very existence of Northern Ireland was called into question.

In Belfast the charge of gerrymandering did not stick. The abolition of proportional representation in local government elections in 1922 simply returned the city to the electoral boundaries drawn up before the First World War, boundaries that had been agreed by Nationalist politicians. Catholics in Belfast were no more unfairly represented in local government than were Conservatives in Ebbw Vale or Labour supporters in Hampshire. The system of patronage, which grew after 1945 with the growth of government, was certainly dominated by Unionists but opposition parties participated with equal enthusiasm: contracts, houses and even the most insignificant jobs such as binmen were given out as favours by all the parties.

The Housing Trust's house building programme and its fair points system of allocation ensured that Catholics benefited in roughly equal proportion to their numbers but this system overlooked the fact that it was mainly Catholics who needed urgent rehousing. Discrimination in employment was a natural product of a divided community and Catholics and Protestants discriminated with equal zeal: given Protestant domination of skilled trades, however, Catholics were at a disadvantage in this game. Both traditional employers and new multinationals were subject to Protestant labour pressure: thus Harland & Wolff, the Sirocco Works and Mackies, despite their proximity to Catholic districts, employed insignificant numbers of Catholics. No figures for relative unemployment levels were compiled during the Stormont years. However, in 1972, when male unemployment in the Belfast urban area was 8.2 per cent, the rate was 19.7 per cent in the lower Falls, 23.7 per cent in Dock, and 33.3 per cent in Ballymurphy.

In 1968 the civil rights campaign was launched in Belfast in earnest by a group of students under the banner People's Democracy (PD). Sit-ins and marches developed into confrontation with the police or Protestant counter-demonstrators. On 5 January 1969, O'Neill said on television, 'Enough is enough. We have heard sufficient for now about civil rights; let us hear a little more about civic responsibility.' But O'Neill had not done enough to satisfy either those seeking change or those frightened by the prospect of change. At the Stormont election of February 1969 traditional unionism fractured into Official and Unofficial Unionist factions, each of which were themselves split between pro-O'Neill and anti-O'Neill candidates. On 28 April 1969 O'Neill resigned as prime minister, claiming that he had 'tried to break the chains of ancient hatreds' but had 'been unable to realise . . . all that I had sought to achieve'. His successor, James Chichester-Clark, announced the introduction of universal suffrage for the next local elections, but events had taken on a momentum of their own and the disturbances continued.

By mid-August raging violence in Derry was raising tensions in Belfast. On the night of 14 August, Catholic youths confronted police and B Specials at Divis Flats while Protestant youths mobilised a short distance away. In the darkness shots rang out and soon gunfire became general. In Divis Street the two mobs clashed repeatedly, with the B Specials, all of whom were Protestants, allegedly helping the Protestant mob. Soon there were riots too in Ardoyne. The army finally separated the combatants with a 'peaceline' of corrugated iron and barbed wire, but by then seven people were dead and 1,820 families, mostly Catholic, had been forced from their homes.

By sending troops for active duty into the streets of Belfast, the British government had made one of the most crucial military decisions since Suez. Hereafter armoured cars, barbed wire and constant foot patrols were to give Belfast the appearance of a war zone.

A series of inquiries and reports initiated by the Westminster parliament alienated loyalists by upholding charges of discrimination against Catholics, depriving the RUC of their arms when on normal duties, and disbanding the B Specials. Fierce riots by loyalists against the RUC and army followed in October 1969. However, the initial enthusiasm of Catholics for the new reserve force, the Ulster Defence Regiment (UDR), and the formation of the Alliance Party, which favoured the Union and reform, and the Social Democratic and Labour Party (SDLP), which gave the minority community a single voice, in early 1970, seemed to offer hope for consensus and political dialogue. Renewed rioting in east Belfast which claimed another six lives, and the first appearance on the streets of the city of a new military force, the Provisional IRA, in June 1970 (following the IRA split at the end of 1969) undermined such optimism. The Provisionals had been formed by those who believed that the traditional IRA had failed to defend Catholics the previous August. In summer 1970 they launched a bombing campaign, with Belfast a prime target, with the aim of forcing Britain to withdraw from Northern Ireland. By early 1971 the Provisionals had murdered British soldiers and brought the violence to a new level of intensity.

Chichester-Clark resigned on 20 March 1971. His successor, Brian Faulkner, was expected to take stronger action against the IRA, and on 9 August he initiated the internment of terrorist suspects. However, the operation failed to remove the most active terrorists or their leaders. Terrible violence erupted and by the end of the month thirty-five people were dead. The destruction of houses and the flight of their occupants was dubbed 'residential displacement' by the official report:

> ... the nature of the movement of population this August has differed greatly from ... August 1969. ... On this occasion the Army 'Peace Line' dividing the strongly

Crumlin Road area, August 1969: 1,820 families fled their homes in the city during that month, 1,505 of them Catholic.
BELFAST TELEGRAPH

> segregated areas appears to have been effective . . . and the major upheaval has transferred to the mixed areas which were formerly thought to serve as 'buffer zones' guaranteeing stability . . .

The vast majority of householders displaced in 1969 had been Catholics but in 1971, 60 per cent were Catholics and 40 per cent were Protestants. Catholics fled from New Ardoyne, Ballysillan, Monkstown, Springfield Road, Donegall Road, Roden Street, Mountpottinger, Bryson Street, Ballybeen and Tullycarnet: Protestants fled from the Farringdon/Cranbrook area of New Ardoyne, Oldpark, New Lodge, the Grosvenor Road, Lanark Street, Mulholland Street, Suffolk, Lenadoon and Bryson Street. Throughout 1971 the Provisionals bombed commercial premises and murdered members of the security forces and innocent Protestants, and loyalists retaliated with horrific attacks on innocent Catholics. The Stormont government was on the verge of collapse.

TROUBLED CITY
1972–96

When, during a demonstration in January 1972, thirteen nationalist protesters in Derry were shot dead by soldiers of the 1st Parachute Regiment, the furious rioting that broke out involving nationalists and security forces spilled over into Belfast. The IRA stepped up its campaign of terror, bombing the Abercorn Restaurant on 3 March when it was crowded with Saturday shoppers, killing 2 people, maiming 4 and injuring 136: on 20 March an explosion in Donegall Street killed 2 policemen and 4 civilians. Westminster now sought direct control of security. When Faulkner's government resigned rather than approve this demand, Edward Heath, the British Prime Minister, announced the suspension of the Stormont government and the beginning of direct rule from Westminster; William Whitelaw was to be the first Secretary of State for

The aftermath of the Abercorn bomb, 3 March 1972
PUBLIC RECORD OFFICE OF NORTHERN IRELAND

Northern Ireland. On 28 March, the final day of the Northern Ireland parliament, Belfast effectively closed down as a huge column of loyalists marched to Stormont in protest.

Meanwhile, the conflict escalated. The IRA detonated twenty-six bombs across Belfast on a single day in July, killing 9 people and injuring 130, while sectarian assassinations, the principal weapon of loyalist paramilitaries, spread fear across the city: 53 people, mainly Catholics, and mainly in Belfast, were killed by loyalists in the final four months of 1972. The population movement continued. In 1973 Westminster made a concerted effort to find a political solution. Proportional representation was used at the district council elections in May in rehearsal for elections in June to a new assembly. This body was to replace the Northern Ireland parliament and was to be run by a twelve-person executive, appointed by the Secretary of State from elected representatives, with the aim of creating a government representing both unionists and nationalists. The resistance of various loyalist parties made the task difficult and the formation of a power-sharing executive, with the former Unionist Prime Minister Faulkner and the SDLP leader Gerry Fitt, as his deputy, at its head, was delayed until November. The Assembly was reinforced by the Sunningdale Agreement between London and Dublin in December which made Irish unification dependent upon the consent of the majority in Northern Ireland and established a Council of Ireland for north–south economic co-operation.

But, the middle ground necessary for such a scheme to succeed did not exist. Terrorism continued unabated with Belfast in the forefront: of the 1,000 deaths recorded by April 1974, 620 had been in the Belfast area.

The United Ulster Unionist Council (UUUC), which rejected Sunningdale and power-sharing, won eleven of the twelve seats at the general election in February 1974, gaining over 50 per cent of the vote.

On 14 May 1974 the Assembly passed an amendment expressing faith in power-sharing by 44 votes to 28. The Ulster Workers' Council (UWC), whose leadership included representatives of loyalist workers in Belfast's heavy industry and power stations as well as loyalist paramilitaries and several prominent Unionist politicians, called a strike for the next day. By 18 May Belfast was experiencing power blackouts of up to six hours, which forced shops and industry to close. Road-blocks manned by loyalist paramilitaries sealed off almost every route to the city centre and for much of the strike most people in Belfast, like those in the rest of Northern Ireland, were deprived of electricity, gas, transport, fresh food, piped water, employment and other facilities taken for granted in any western European state. Lieutenant-General Sir Frank King had 17,500 troops under his command but he decided that to intervene would be disastrous: 'if you get a large section of the population which is bent on a particular course then it is a difficult thing to stop them'. When troops took over the principal petrol stations in Belfast on 27 May the UWC responded by reducing electricity supplies to 10 per cent of capacity and withdrawing workers from essential services. Faulkner, unable to persuade his SDLP allies to negotiate with the strikers, resigned the next day – the power-sharing experiment was at an end. Loyalists celebrated by lighting bonfires across the city. One of the most effective general strikes in Western Europe since 1945 had come to an end.

The strike forced local people to organise a plethora

of community groups to provide food and other essentials, as well as alternative social services when official services were paralysed. However, it was the local authority and government agencies that had to cope with the more enduring problem of social need. The inefficient division of Belfast's welfare services between three authorities was ended in October 1973 with the establishment of the Eastern Health and Social Services Board (EHSSB) covering the greater Belfast area. Of the EHSSB's five districts, North and West Belfast was the biggest, containing a population of 250,000; it was also the poorest. Peter Townsend's study *Poverty in the United Kingdom*, published in 1979 but based on research carried out ten years earlier, compared deprived areas in Belfast with those in Glasgow, Salford and Neath.

> With the exception of Neath, the percentage found to be in poverty ... was high being 38 for selected areas of Salford, 48 for Glasgow Shettleton, and 50 for Belfast. The figure for the UK as a whole was 28.

A government report, *Belfast Areas of Special Social Need* (1977), identified 'two major need syndromes':

> One is characterised by unemployment, low incomes and overcrowded housing resulting from large family size. This has a West Belfast distribution. The other is an inner city syndrome, distinguished by sub-standard housing, poor physical environment, low incomes, lack of skills and concentrations of persons with different forms of physical handicap whether associated with age or health.

The North and West district was not only an area of high rates of adult male and long-term unemployment, bad housing, educational underachievement and juvenile delinquency, but also the front line in the communal conflict; fifty killings took place there in 1976 alone. The 1978 Belfast Household Survey showed that 70,000 people (19 per cent of the city's population) had left Belfast since 1971. Despite depopulation the number of people chasing jobs still far outweighed the job opportunities available and unemployment rates in mainly Catholic districts such as Clonard, Court, Falls, Grosvenor, Milltown, New Lodge and Whiterock remained stubbornly high, ranging from 22 to 35 per cent, compared with 9 per cent in the city as a whole.

Housing remained in crisis. Between 1969 and 1976, 25,000 houses were destroyed or damaged by explosions; homes abandoned by fleeing families were often vandalised, and in Belfast alone, 9,000 were irreparably damaged or boarded up. The Stormont and Westminster governments had agreed in 1969 to remove housing from local authority control and to administer it through a central agency, the Northern Ireland Housing Executive (NIHE); this became operational in 1971. The NIHE's task was complicated by the rent and rates strike undertaken in protest against internment by 22,000 tenants in nationalist areas in 1971–72, by a shortage of skilled workers willing to work in conflict areas, and by the reluctance of Westminster to pay for new dwellings. But the new organisation's greatest problem was that it was, in the words of one government minister, 'the largest slum landlord in Europe'. An NIHE survey in 1974 revealed that in the Belfast urban area 24.2 per cent of all dwellings (29,750 in all) were officially unfit for human habitation; in the inner city area west of the Lagan, half the houses were unfit – 32.4 per cent of these had no inside toilet. A holding operation was initiated, with grants for improvements being made available.

The Housing Executive's work was further

Northern Ireland Housing Executive redevelopment in the Markets area, with St Malachy's Church in the background.

hampered by the grandiose schemes of the 1960s, when in the context of cheap energy and economic expansion plans were drawn up for the M1 and M2 motorways, for the Matthew Plan and the Belfast Urban Motorway, and for the new city of Craigavon. It was estimated that 74,500 new homes would be needed in the Belfast urban area by 1981 but that there were sites for only 47,500 within the boundaries set on new housing: 27,000 families would have to move out to designated growth areas. Few in office thought of asking the people who were to have their homes demolished if they wanted to leave.

The urban motorway was to cut a swathe through the densely packed areas of Sandy Row, the lower Falls and the lower Shankill, and local discontent soon mobilised opposition. In particular, the Protestant community in the Shankill felt threatened with extinction as only a small proportion of families could be re-housed locally. Protests forced the abandonment of plans to build urban motorway flyovers and fifteen-storey flats, but the Westlink and the medium-rise 'Weetabix' blocks completed in 1974 were equally effective in destroying the sense of community in the area. In contrast the Divis Flats complex in the Falls, completed in 1972, was initially welcomed by locals who wanted to stay in the area. By 1979 the level of unfit stock in Belfast had fallen to 15 per cent but the problems associated with high-rise dwellings everywhere, exacerbated by the shoddy construction of some developments, led to further campaigns by tenants.

Following the failure of power-sharing, and negotiations with the IRA, the Labour government called elections in May 1975 to a Constitutional Convention, whose remit was to consider what arrangement for the government of Northern Ireland was 'likely to command the most widespread acceptance' there. The UUUC again won a majority of seats, both in Belfast and throughout Northern Ireland, and the Convention

The abiding media image of 1970s Belfast: soldiers, barbed wire and children, Docks area, 1975
BELFAST CENTRAL LIBRARY

report thus recommended a return to majority rule. This was rejected by the government and the prospects for a political settlement receded.

Continued violence filled the void but one incident in August 1976, when an IRA getaway car whose driver had just been shot dead at the wheel by a British soldier crashed into and killed three of Mrs Anne Maguire's four children, shocked people into action. Mrs Maguire's sister, Mairead Corrigan, and Betty Williams, who had witnessed the tragedy, and Ciaran McKeown founded the Peace People. Similar groups, such as Women Together and Protestant and Catholic Encounter (PACE), had been preaching reconciliation for years, but this group captured the imagination and for its efforts won the Nobel Peace Prize in 1977. Despite such international plaudits the Peace People's popularity in Belfast proved ephemeral: they were prophets with least honour in their own city.

In 1977–78 IRA attacks on the security forces were supplemented by a firebomb campaign against commercial premises, the most gruesome of which at the La Mon House Hotel killed twelve people. In response, loyalist paramilitaries continued their murder campaign, while many Protestants turned to the Reverend Ian Paisley for more vigorous political leadership: at the May 1979 general election his Democratic Unionist Party (DUP) won North and East Belfast from the Ulster Unionists and in June he topped the poll at the first European parliament elections. Paisley's failure to mobilise much support for another loyalist strike in 1977 and Catholic revulsion against IRA atrocities such as La Mon House were deceptive – the new Conservative government would have to deal with a Belfast that was as deeply divided as ever.

In 1981, following a hunger strike in the Maze Prison, near Lisburn, in which ten republican prisoners died, the republican movement developed a new strategy, sometimes called 'the armalite and the ballot box'. The election shortly before his death of one of the hunger strikers, Bobby Sands, as MP for Fermanagh–South Tyrone and the huge attendance at his funeral in Belfast in May 1981 convinced Sinn Féin, the IRA's political wing, that widespread sympathy within Catholic areas should be harnessed to their cause. The IRA's murder of the Reverend Robert Bradford, MP for South Belfast, in November 1981, served as a reminder of the limitations of this new-found zeal for elections. Both Sinn Féin and the SDLP contested the October 1982 elections to a new Northern Ireland assembly, but both refused to participate, rejecting such 'internal solutions'. Sinn Féin's 10 per cent of first preference votes threatened the SDLP's position as the main nationalist party. Nowhere was this more evident than in Belfast, where Sinn Féin won two council by-elections in 1983 and 1984 and Gerry Adams won West Belfast at the Westminster election in 1983. London and Dublin were jolted into political consultations designed to halt this trend.

Political unrest did nothing to help Belfast's economy. When Grundig closed its Dunmurry plant in 1980 the management admitted that one reason it had done so was the existence of 'disturbances of a political nature', reinforcing analyses that the Troubles had cost Northern Ireland around 20,000–30,000 jobs in the 1970s. Economic decline would have taken place, however, even in a peaceful environment. The decay of Belfast's old staple industries, such as shipbuilding and engineering, meant that the 65,000 new industrial jobs created by 1970, mostly in the Belfast region, merely absorbed the impact of job losses in these older industries rather than reducing unemployment levels. In 1973 the oil crisis undermined one of the Belfast region's most important new industries, synthetic fibre production.

The recession of 1979–83 further whittled away Belfast's manufacturing base, and the government's prestige project, the US-owned De Lorean car company in Dunmurry, designed to bring employment to west Belfast, was forced to close in 1982. Those companies that survived cut their workforces. Harland & Wolff employed only 5,163 people by 1985 compared to 7,542 in 1979. The economic crisis was exacerbated by cuts in public expenditure which deprived the construction industry of its supply of government projects and temporarily halted the growth in service jobs. Only massive government subventions allowed both Shorts Brothers and Harland & Wolff to compete in the new global market, the former winning a £460 million contract for Sherpa freighter aircraft for its 6,600-strong workforce in 1984, the latter in the same year securing a £110 million contract for a Single Well Oil Production ship from British Petroleum. The two companies accounted for around 10 per cent of all manufacturing employment, and received one third of all public resources going to industrial support. Despite 'fair employment' legislation and the efforts of management to implement this and produce a neutral working environment, the workforces of both Shorts and Harland & Wolff remained overwhelmingly Protestant.

The housing regeneration programme was threatened by the Thatcher government's public spending cuts. Charles Brett, the NIHE chairman, convinced

Panoramic view of Belfast city centre following an explosion in Chichester Street, 1980
PUBLIC RECORD OFFICE OF NORTHERN IRELAND

ministers that spending money on housing would do more good than anything else to boost the local economy, and in 1981 the government made housing its first social priority. By the mid-1980s the NIHE's capital programme reached £100 million a year and its workforce numbered around 5,000. The development of Poleglass on the periphery of southwest Belfast, begun in 1980, was continued; neighbouring Twinbrook extended west Belfast into the Lisburn council area. Both developments were instrumental in allowing west Belfast to retain its Catholic, nationalist character, a fact much resented by Protestants from the Shankill who, lacking the skills and coherence of their Catholic counterparts in organising pressure groups to change the government's mind, had been forced to move to satellite towns such as Newtownabbey and Carrickfergus.

The Troubles forced Belfast to show its resilience and

to develop formidable recuperative powers. Buses and the postal service were attacked regularly during the early 1970s yet both continued to operate their services. Local 'black taxi' services emerged on the Falls and Shankill roads, creating employment and providing a cheaper and more reliable service than the buses. Bomb damage in the city forced some establishments, such as the Grand Central, Midland and Russell Court hotels, to close down, but others, such as the Europa Hotel and the Co-operative department store, rebuilt their businesses. Moreover, new stores such as Marks & Spencer, Boots and Dunne's replaced those that had been lost. The city centre was pedestrianised, protected by security barriers and searchers, and enhanced by ornate street furniture and flowers. A plethora of leisure centres was opened by the City Council, and they, together with the expansion of the health services at the Royal Victoria, Ulster, Musgrave Park and City hospitals, the building of new schools, and the development of further education at the colleges of business and technology, provided considerable social improvements.

Cultural life remained surprisingly vigorous if decidedly middle class. The Queen's University Festival, developed by Michael Emmerson and Michael Barnes in the mid-1960s, attracted performers of international repute and developed into the largest festival outside Edinburgh, whilst the youthful Ulster Orchestra grew and flourished. Arts Council funding allowed the Lyric Theatre to modernise and the Arts Theatre to reopen, the Queen's festival to expand, and new publishing houses – Blackstaff and Appletree – to open. Talented writers such as Martin Lynch from Turf Lodge and Graham Reid from the 'Village' in the Donegall Road provided the theatres with stimulating plays; Reid's highly acclaimed 'Billy' plays for BBC Northern Ireland showcased the talents of another young Belfast man, Kenneth Branagh. But the mingling of Belfast's Protestant and Catholic middle classes at the theatre and at golf clubs such as Balmoral and Malone could not bridge the huge political gulf that still existed.

In 1985 Sinn Féin won seven city council seats compared to the SDLP's six. London and Dublin intensified their search for a political agreement that would reverse this trend and this in turn brought the two main Unionist parties closer together. The Anglo-Irish Agreement which emerged from the consultations created a joint ministerial conference of British and Irish ministers, backed by a joint secretariat of civil servants at Maryfield, near Belfast, to monitor political, legal and other issues of concern to nationalists. It stated that the government's aim was devolution of power to a body having 'widespread acceptance'. But despite the agreement's recognition of the constitutional status quo, Unionists were furious both with the content of the agreement and with the fact that they had not been consulted while the SDLP clearly had had an input. On 23 November, James Molyneaux and Ian Paisley addressed a huge crowd of unionist supporters, possibly numbering 200,000, outside Belfast City Hall in protest at the agreement and to initiate a campaign of 'passive resistance'.

In December, loyalist shipyard and aircraft workers downed tools and marched on Maryfield but there was no repeat of 1974: the agreement had created no devolved structure for loyalists to tear down. Frustrations boiled over into ugly attacks upon the predominantly Protestant police who were deemed to be

A massive unionist protest against the Anglo-Irish Agreement, City Hall, 23 November 1985.
BELFAST TELEGRAPH

upholding the agreement and betraying Northern Ireland. The thirteen Unionist MPs resigned their seats and forced by-elections in January 1986, in order to provide their supporters with an opportunity to voice their opposition. Belfast returned its three Unionist MPs, but overall unionist support fell short of the 500,000 votes target by more than 80,000; Sinn Féin's share of the nationalist vote fell from 41.9 per cent to 35.4 per cent, indicating to the two governments that their strategy was working and should not be changed. Loyalist anger grew and a 'day of action' was called for 3 March 1986. Public services and industry were disrupted by barricades on main roads and by power cuts. In Belfast, gangs of youths rampaged through the city centre and shots were fired at the police during riots that evening in loyalist enclaves. The Reverend Martin Smyth, MP for South Belfast, condemned such attacks as the Unionist leaders strove to retain control of a volatile situation.

A new, more moderate strategy was developed, based on non-cooperation with government, and including MPs absenting themselves from Westminster and the disruption of local government business. Sammy Wilson, Belfast's new DUP mayor, succeeded in continuing a selective non-cooperation strategy in the council until February 1987 when a High Court fine of £25,000 punctured such resistance. Loyalist reaction was sometimes farcical, such as the incident in August 1987 when Peter Robinson, MP for East Belfast, 'invaded' a village in the Republic of Ireland with five hundred supporters, but it could also be lethal: paramilitary attacks on Catholics, especially in north Belfast, began to increase. With IRA actions against British forces also escalating in reaction to what Adams called 'the agreement . . . stabilising British interests', Belfast's future looked bleak.

At the general election in June 1987, Adams held on to his West Belfast seat but the SDLP retained its position as the dominant nationalist party in Northern Ireland. New IRA tactics such as the murder of contractors working for the security forces had clearly repulsed many. At the same time the security forces were penetrating the IRA's cell network, killing eight members at Loughgall in May 1986 and seizing weapons from the *Eksund*'s cargo ship in October 1987. In response the IRA focused operations on Britain and Europe. When British special forces shot dead an IRA team in Gibraltar in March 1988, the three bodies were brought to Belfast for martyrs' funerals. On 16 March at Milltown cemetery, a lone loyalist, Michael Stone, fired shots and threw grenades at the crowd, killing three people. Only three days later, at the funeral of one of those killed two British soldiers drove into the gathering mourners. When challenged by stewards they brandished a gun and attempted to reverse at speed but a furious mob, suspecting another loyalist attack, surrounded the vehicle and dragged the men out: they were brutally beaten, and after they were discovered to be plainclothes soldiers, they were shot dead. Both funerals were captured by television cameras and did much to reinforce the worldwide perception of Belfast as a city of savage violence.

Over the next two years the IRA continued its campaign against British targets in Northern Ireland, Britain and Europe. In Belfast City Hall Unionists found the presence of Sinn Féin councillors hard to bear. When a leading republican objected to the closure of St George's Market in June 1988 he was greeted with shouts of 'Gangsters, IRA men, get them out' and an appeal to the chair asking, 'Is it in order to appeal to keep the market open when his party blew it up?'; the Sinn Féin reply, 'You never know, it could be bombed again', reinforced Unionist suspicions that republicans were simply using democratic politics as another weapon in the conflict. Throughout the 1980s the loyalist paramilitary organisations had been comparatively inactive, concentrating their efforts on racketeering and gangsterism, but around 1989–90 young militants within the Ulster Defence Association (UDA) and the Ulster Volunteer Force (UVF) took control. Stating their frustration at the inability of the security forces to defeat the IRA and angered by Sinn Féin's bravado, they purchased modern weapons and began a murder campaign against republicans. Eighteen people with Sinn Féin connections, including three Sinn Féin councillors and the son of a councillor, were shot dead over a five-year period. They also indiscriminately murdered Catholics with no republican involvement; these included six taxi drivers killed in Belfast in the space of fifteen months.

Westminster again searched for a political formula that would undermine the terrorists. In February 1991 Peter Brooke, the new Secretary of State for Northern Ireland, initiated 'talks about talks' between the constitutional parties, prompting the loyalist paramilitaries to call a ceasefire. This lasted until the talks collapsed in July and the sectarian murders started once again. The IRA responded by murdering twelve Protestants between April and November 1991, with Belfast the main killing ground. The city also suffered at the hands of the IRA's bombing campaign. In the winter of 1991–92 Musgrave Park Hospital, the Law Courts and surrounding businesses, the Plaza and Europa hotels and the Grand Opera House were all severely damaged. Two massive bombs inflicted millions of pounds' worth of damage on businesses in Bedford Street and High Street. The security forces' counter-operation, with the 'approaches to Belfast and roads to the city centre ... cordoned by vehicle checkpoints, operating around the clock', was designed to reassure the public and maintain normal life in the city centre, but it was 'not normal to find street after street brought to a dead-end with white security tape; to pass so many "business as usual" signs on window-boarded premises'.

Following the IRA's murder of eight Protestant workmen at Teebane, County Tyrone, Belfast's DUP mayor, Nigel Dodds, refused to greet the President of the Republic of Ireland, Mary Robinson, when she visited the city on 3 February 1992. The next day an off-duty RUC man killed three men in Sinn Féin's Falls Road offices and later turned his gun on himself. Two days later loyalists claiming they were exacting revenge for Teebane murdered five Catholics in a betting shop on the Ormeau Road. A general election was scheduled for April and the IRA was determined to keep the constitutional question on the political agenda: Belfast suffered two large bombs in March as the Provisionals intensified their campaign against economic targets. At the April poll, Belfast's three Unionist MPs were re-elected but in West Belfast tactical voting by unionists enabled Dr Joe Hendron of the SDLP to oust Gerry Adams, despite the latter's increased vote. The election was followed by a massive IRA bomb blast in London's financial centre. The continuing death toll and the economic cost of conflict in Northern Ireland and in Britain increased the urgency of efforts to produce a new political initiative.

Early in 1983 a political scientist had characterised Belfast as 'ugly and sore to the eye, the will to go on gone... a modern wasteland'. He added: 'Only the ghettoes have their own vitality. By early evening Belfast is abandoned.' The *Observer*, in 1984, reported that Belfast's 'poverty is ancient and ingrained'. Yet

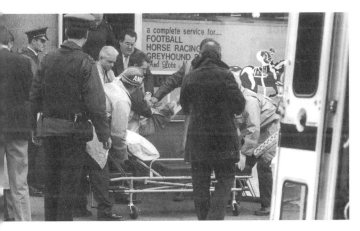

Sean Graham's betting shop, Ormeau Road, February 1992; five Catholics were killed by two UFF gunmen.
BELFAST TELEGRAPH

even as these impressions were being written, the transformation of Belfast had begun. IRA bombings in the city centre decreased considerably in the 1980s and paramilitary crime was more effectively countered. A *Belfast Telegraph* article in May 1985 enthused that 'an outsider who had not visited the city for two or three years would notice the difference right away'. There was 'a new buzz and bustle about a city that looks better, smells better and smiles better'.

The city council developed an advertising campaign based on this theme, trumpeting the slogan 'Belfast's got the buzz' to reattract visitors and shoppers. No longer subjected to body searches, citizens were able to pour in and out of the security gates at will. Bright shops and boutiques blossomed, and flower tubs, thousands of trees, new paving and modern lamp standards adorned the streets. Between 1982 and 1985 some 41 restaurants, 38 cafés and 55 hot-food bars opened, while around £86 million was invested in commercial development in the inner-city area.

A great deal of the regeneration was government-funded and by the end of the decade a succession of post-modernist commercial premises and office blocks dominated the skyline. The showpiece of the 1989 Belfast Urban Plan was the Laganside scheme to transform around 300 acres of the port's waterfront into a tourist and leisure complex. This included the city council's ambitious Laganbank development of a concert hall, ice rink, hotel, marina, harbour village and business village. Although the recession of the early 1990s damaged private investment, forcing the Laganside scheme to be restructured and leaving much of the new office space in Great Victoria Street unlet, the regeneration continued. Even the IRA's renewed bombing

144

campaign of 1991–92 failed to drive out shoppers and those seeking entertainment. Marks & Spencer's Belfast store became one of the company's most lucrative branches; the Castle Court shopping complex brought major retail outlets to the city; the new MGM Movie House provided a ten-screen cinema; and after the bomb of December 1991, the Grand Opera House simply moved its Christmas pantomime to La Mon House, repaired the damage and reopened in April 1992.

Nevertheless, the heavily fortified army and police bases which continued to mar the Belfast landscape stood as stark reminders that this was no ordinary city. For many nationalists the bases were symbols of Belfast's problems rather than part of a solution. Castlereagh holding centre in east Belfast, where terrorist suspects were interviewed, was alleged to torture detainees and was investigated by Amnesty International. It was seen as part of a deeper conspiracy between the security forces and loyalist paramilitaries. However, despite celebrated cases of such 'collusion', the efforts of the RUC to maintain its impartiality remained high, a fact well illustrated by the arrest and conviction of one of the most ruthless loyalist commanders, Johnny 'Mad Dog' Adair.

The government was determined to counter the polarising effects of terrorism by providing Northern Ireland's citizens with infrastructural, social and economic improvements. This stood in marked contrast to the Thatcher government's cuts in public expenditure in Britain. The Economic Council summed up the disparity in 1989:

Public expenditure in Northern Ireland (excluding social security) has grown by about 1.3 per cent per annum in real terms over the past five years. This compares with an average annual decrease nationally of approximately 0.5 per cent.

Writing in the *Guardian* that same year, Ian Aitken referred to the region as 'the Independent Keynesian Republic of Northern Ireland'. Nowhere were such projects more important than in Belfast.

The demolition of the unpopular medium-rise flats at Divis and the Shankill, the building of attractive replacement houses and the redevelopment of Unity Flats, meant that by 1987 Belfast's housing crisis was well on its way to being solved. Employment, therefore, became the government's priority, and a myriad of agencies played a role. The Industrial Development Board (IDB, dealing with large, often overseas companies) and the Local Enterprise Development Unit (LEDU, dealing with smaller, local companies) achieved much in the 1980s, the former bringing inward investment to Northern Ireland by providing attractive grants and factory infrastructure. By 1989, government employment schemes accounted for a quarter of all jobs in industry while the employment of the remainder in manufacturing was heavily dependent on government subsidy; the largest employment growth sector, services, accounted for nearly two thirds of Northern Ireland's jobs by 1985 and of these, 60 per cent were public sector jobs in the civil service, government agencies and local government. Not surprisingly, such massive subventions led to accusations that Northern Ireland had a 'workhouse economy', reliant upon public expenditure, in which those not unemployed mainly spent their time providing services and administration rather than producing saleable products.

When the largest concerns, Shorts and Harland & Wolff, were privatised in 1989 it cost the taxpayer £986 million and £500 million respectively. The two companies faced stiff competition in the global market. Harland & Wolff pared its workforce to around 2,000 and Shorts shed over 2,000 jobs between 1994 and 1996, though with around 6,000 employees it remained Northern Ireland's largest employer. Shorts spent £200 million on modernisation and, supported by £22.5 million from the IDB, designed and built the airframe for the Learjet 45. The highs and lows of global competition were demonstrated in early 1996 when Harland & Wolff won a major contract to build floating production, storage and off-loading vessels (FPSOs) as Shorts faced the prospect of hundreds of job losses when a major client, Fokker, closed.

The recession of the early 1990s meant that fewer new investors were attracted, though what new jobs there were helped to avoid the severe job losses suffered by British manufacturing during this period. Between 1991 and 1995, ten of the IDB's forty investment projects plus several advance factories were sited in the greater Belfast area, thanks to the government's policy of targeting social need; they created approximately 1,200 jobs. The Training and Employment Agency addresses 75 per cent (£130 million) of its budget to areas with 'problems of social need' such as the Shankill where 85 per cent of the working-age population are without qualifications. And another new agency, Making Belfast Work (MBW), is spending £25 million a year on improving the social environment in north and west Belfast and the inner-city regions east and west of the Lagan, and on providing residents there with education and training to enable them to compete in the job market. This huge network of grants and subsidies operated by nonelected bodies responsible to government ministers has been the subject of much debate. Unionist politicians complain that nationalist areas are receiving disproportionately more per head than unionist areas and that city councillors such as themselves should be taking the decisions rather than government appointees. Nationalist politicians lobby the government to maintain the present system, castigating unionist suggestions as an effort to return to the Stormont years and unionist domination of employment contracts and housing. Nationalists also argue that unionists fail to take into account the greater social need in nationalist areas. Among the suburban middle class, however, there are rumblings of discontent about spending such huge sums on 'the people who keep all the trouble going'. It remains to be seen whether an enterprise culture can be created where a dependency culture now exists.

In March 1988 *The Economist* magazine claimed that one Northern Ireland minister 'used to escort parties of English MPs round the province to show them its problems' but he 'found them so envious of his bailiwick's housing and health that he stopped inviting them'. Spending per head on housing was three times greater in Northern Ireland than in England and Wales in 1986–87; in 1990 Northern Ireland had 10 per cent of its gross domestic product spent on health care compared to 6 per cent in England; and while spending on education in Britain fell throughout the 1980s, Northern Ireland's total real expenditure on education began to rise after 1986. However, social security reform meant that Thatcherism did make an impact. In 1987, 27 per cent of households were living on supplementary benefit, many of these in Belfast. The introduction of the Social Security Act in 1988 replaced supplementary benefit with Income Support and substituted loans for the grants previously available for essential items such as beds and cookers; consequently, dependent families suffered increased difficulties. For those in higher income brackets, however, improvements in infrastructure and services were welcome.

Belfast has not suffered traffic congestion on the scale of British cities and the Roads Service is piloting a range of schemes, such as 'park 'n' ride' cycle routes and bus priority on radial routes, to ensure it does not in future. The new M3 motorway link, giving easier access to the northern and eastern satellite towns, and the cross-harbour road and rail link, have also helped. Flyovers at the Westlink and the new Stockman's Lane junction, to be built at a cost of £20 million by the year 2000, will help unblock other bottlenecks. The new Central and Great Victoria Street stations have improved the cohesion of the rail network, and the Sydenham stop provides a linking to the expanding City Airport. Like Aldergrove International Airport, the City Airport has expanded considerably its range of flights within the British Isles and further afield.

Signs of belated Thatcherism, such as the proposal to seek private finance for road building, are also evident in other areas. The Royal Victoria Hospital is earmarked for a £645 million redevelopment, but it has had to fight hard to keep its maternity unit, and cutbacks seem certain to affect other hospitals such as Musgrave Park. In social services, home helps have had working hours squeezed to the point of industrial action. The city council has approved plans to sell several areas of parkland to raise capital and is searching for private investment to help establish an environmental protection zone in the Belfast hills. Both Queen's University and the University of Ulster at Jordanstown, like many British universities, face financial difficulties, whilst schools will lose teachers in 1996. Consultations on plans to set up a new £15 million university campus at Springvale, straddling the peaceline in west Belfast, are ongoing, but the scheme has been condemned by some as a headline-grabbing political venture rather than a necessary educational step. Indeed, many commentators feel that government spending has been driven by political considerations: improvements such as new houses could give people renewed hope and undermine the appeal of the terrorist. It is a theory reinforced by the government's commitment to community relations.

In 1981 Lagan College was established in east Belfast by local people seeking to create an integrated education system in which Catholics and Protestants would be taught side by side. The government approved efforts to promote mutual understanding but remained aloof. However, the introduction of the national curriculum in 1989 allowed the government to make a financial commitment to integrated schooling and to institutionalise programmes such as Education for Mutual Understanding (EMU) and Cultural Heritage across the entire primary and secondary education system. Pupils were to study the extent to which their heritage was shared, diverse and distinctive, whilst schools that arranged cross-community projects, such as trips, were to receive EMU funding. The Hazelwood schools in north Belfast provided a complete integrated education from primary to secondary level. School leavers could come together at the two universities or at the new

Belfast Institute of Further and Higher Education, created in 1991 by the amalgamation of the city's three colleges. Awareness amongst adults has been promoted by the Cultural Traditions group since 1988 and in 1990 the Community Relations Council was established to underwrite local efforts to bridge the sectarian divide. Such efforts, however, touched only a few. At Queen's University, Protestants objected to the dropping of the British national anthem which had previously been played at graduation ceremonies, whilst Catholics continued to complain of discrimination in employment. Belfast's divisions remained deep, divisions that only a political settlement could hope to bridge.

The talks process designed to produce such a settlement restarted in Belfast in March 1992 and continued until the following November. It involved the British and Irish governments and the main political parties in Northern Ireland with the exception of Sinn Féin, and bilateral discussions between the parties and the new Secretary of State, Sir Patrick Mayhew, continued subsequently. Nevertheless, the failure of the parties to reach agreement was dispiriting in the context of ongoing, indeed intensifying, terrorism. Loyalist paramilitaries, operating under the umbrella command structure of the Combined Loyalist Military Command (CLMC), were killing more people than the IRA. Many attacks were sectarian but loyalists claimed the bombing campaign against the homes of Sinn Féin and SDLP activists was designed to destroy the 'pan-nationalist front'.

Consultations between SDLP leader John Hume and Gerry Adams, begun in 1988, became public knowledge by 1992. Hume's aim was to convince republicans to give up violence but loyalists and some unionists feared the Hume–Adams talks would tempt the government into an appeasement policy: the Union would be sacrificed to silence IRA guns, thus fulfilling the nationalist agenda of both Hume and Adams. Loyalist violence was designed to prevent a 'pan-nationalist' victory by showing the government that the Hume–Adams strategy would not bring peace.

In October 1993 the IRA tried to kill the CLMC's leadership by planting a bomb in a Shankill Road fish shop underneath their meeting room. The bomb exploded prematurely, killing nine innocent Protestants and a bomber. Belfast's atmosphere of regeneration was paralysed by the fear of loyalist reprisal; in the week that followed, 13 people were killed by loyalists, including 7 shot dead in a UDA attack on a pub in Greysteel, County Londonderry. Northern Ireland seemed poised to return to the destruction of the 1970s. Revelations that the British government had had secret contacts with republicans reinforced loyalist paranoia and forced London and Dublin to give reassurance that they wanted a settlement acceptable to all parties. This came in December 1993 with the Downing Street Declaration which offered something for everyone: it also stated that any party with a democratic mandate that

Sinn Féin president, Gerry Adams, addressing a rally in west Belfast on the day the IRA announced its ceasefire, 31 August 1994.
BELFAST TELEGRAPH

The loyalist ceasefire announced on 13 October 1994 catapulted David Ervine of the PUP and Gary McMichael of the UDP (second and third from the left respectively) into the media spotlight.
BELFAST TELEGRAPH

established a commitment to peace and democracy would be admitted to the talks process. Thousands backed the peace poll organised by the *News Letter*, *Belfast Telegraph* and *Irish News*; schoolchildren, students, trade unionists and ordinary individuals held rally after rally outside the City Hall demanding peace.

Tempted by the prospect of talks, the IRA called a ceasefire on 31 August 1994. Cavalcades of republicans paraded through west Belfast throughout the day. Loyalists called their own ceasefire on 13 October, catapulting the Progressive Unionist Party (PUP) and the Ulster Democratic Party (UDP), representing the UVF and UDA respectively, into the media spotlight. The atmosphere in Belfast changed: nightlife became confident and vibrant; the number of foreign voices in the streets was noticeable as tourism flourished; and Christmas shopping without security checks on bags felt unusual but welcome.

Both loyalists and republicans met government officials but the key question was how to create confidence and trust amongst the parties so that talks could begin. On 7 March 1995, in a speech in Washington, Sir

United States president, Bill Clinton, speaking at Mackies' foundry during his November 1995 visit to Ireland, emphasised the need for peace, reconciliation and reconstruction.
BELFAST TELEGRAPH

Patrick Mayhew declared that the government believed the only way to convince some parties of the sincerity of the paramilitaries was for the latter to decommission some weapons as a sign of good faith. Months of posturing followed as the process stalled on this issue. But many people were enjoying the peace too much to notice. In 1991 Belfast had organised a year of spectacular events which culminated in the Tall Ships festival, but the shadow of terrorism had always hung over proceedings. Celebrations in May and September 1995 commemorating the Allied victories in Europe and the Far East in the Second World War were the most enjoyable and carefree anyone could remember.

President Clinton's visit in November 1995 enjoyed the same warm atmosphere. His tour of Mackies, his impromptu walkabouts on the Shankill and Falls and his visit to the East Belfast Enterprise Park brought rapturous applause from those present: the tens of thousands at the City Hall to see him switch on the

Christmas lights – to a musical accompaniment provided by the most famous Belfast entertainer alive, Van Morrison – were ecstatic. Belfast was drunk on peace. In reality, however, the President's visit was a veneer covering serious cracks in the peace process; cracks that the two governments' proposals for talks and decommissioning to proceed in parallel could not repair. Paramilitary activity, such as robberies, punishment beatings and even murders, had never completely disappeared after August 1994 but the public had convinced itself that such incidents were ephemeral and not central to the peace process. Consequently, when the IRA ended its ceasefire by exploding a massive bomb in London on 9 February 1996, killing two people, the shock was enormous.

Since February 1996 the people of Belfast have been hoping for a renewed ceasefire and praying that the violence witnessed in Britain does not return to their streets. They have also been voting for delegates to a Forum, electing the traditional spread of candidates. Talks began on 10 June 1996 without Sinn Féin, who

Members of the Ulster Unionist Party arriving at Stormont for all-party talks; foreground, left to right: John Taylor, Reg Empey, David Trimble and Ken Maginnis.

are barred until the IRA ceasefire is reinstated. Whether or not the talks mark the beginning of a bright new future remains to be seen: IRA activity notwithstanding, the sectarian confrontations between the Protestant Orange Order and Catholic residents' groups on the lower Ormeau Road show how difficult it will be for some people to sacrifice tradition to reconciliation. But if the talks do indeed betoken a new beginning, Belfast can expect to retain the special status that has attracted so much government and international funding in recent years for some time to come as the transition to agreed political structures is consolidated. The opportunity to deal in a climate of peace with the same everyday problems that confront other European cities is a challenge the people of Belfast desire and deserve.

Downtown Belfast in the 1990s
BELFAST TELEGRAPH

INDEX

163